Ecli|
Comparativ

A SCENE BY SCENE GUIDE

# Amy Farrell

SCENE BY SCENE
WICKLOW, IRELAND

Scene by Scene
Wicklow, Ireland.
www.scenebyscene.ie

Eclipsed Comparative Study Guide by Amy Farrell.
ISBN 978-1-910949-77-1

Cover Image © Evgenyi Gromov

# Contents

# About This Book

This book is a companion guide for the Comparative Study of *Eclipsed*, by Patricia Burke Brogan. Ideally it accompanies a second, detailed viewing and study of the play.

Each chapter contains notes on Cultural Context/Social Setting, Literary Genre, General Vision and Viewpoint, Theme/Issue - Relationships and Hero/Heroine/Villain, and a set of questions on Cultural Context/Social Setting, Literary Genre, General Vision and Viewpoint, Theme/Issue - Relationships and Hero/Heroine/Villain. The notes are intended as a starting point for students, to provide something concrete for each mode that can be developed and built on by exploring the relevant mode-based questions.

For Hero/Heroine/Villain, Brigit has been selected as the main character to study. However, in scenes where she does not appear, other characters have been selected.

Towards the back of the book, there are notes looking at each mode as a whole, across the entire play, and accompanying questions. (Please note, there may be some similarity with earlier questions to draw attention to key ideas).

Lastly, there is a section of questions on each mode, designed to prompt comparisons between *Eclipsed* and other Comparative Study texts.

# Prologue - Act 1, Scene 1

Set in 1992, Rosa has come to the laundry hoping to find out something about her mother.

## Cultural Context/Social Setting

The play takes place inside a convent-laundry run by nuns, where penitent women (unmarried mothers) are incarcerated.

The large, battered ledger records the details of the laundry's penitent women. Note how many were signed in by their parents, and the number who gave birth to stillborn babies.

1.      Describe the setting.

2.      What does Rosa read from the ledger?
What does this tell you about this place?

3.      "Signed in by her parents..."
What does this tell you about this world?
Would you expect modern-day parents to act the same way?
Fully explain your point of view.

4.      What are your first impressions of this place?
Give reasons for your answer.

# Literary Genre

The setting of this convent-laundry is established in this scene. It is 1992, and Rosa has come to the laundry hoping to learn something about her birth mother, Brigit Murphy. Her search frames the story.

The use of music is very powerful as this scene begins. The sung line, "He was despised. Despised and rejected. Rejected of men," speaks of exclusion and rejection, and the position of the penitent women, incarcerated in the convent-laundry.

The shadowy scene, and the presence of the women behind the drapes, is eerie and atmospheric.

It is moving when Rosa looks at the old photos and discovers one of herself as a baby and reads the details of the women signed into the laundry and the babies they had. Thus, the story of these women, and Rosa's desire to know more, is what sparks the action of the play, taking the audience on a journey into the laundry's past.

1.    What does the setting tell you about the story?

2.    How are the characters dressed?
      What does this communicate to the audience?

3.    What does the use of music add to the scene?

4.    What is happening as the story begins?

5.    What is the effect of seeing figures behind
      shadowy drapes in this scene?

6.      What does Rosa read from the ledger?

         What is the effect of this on the audience?

         How does this make you feel?

7.      What interests you in this story as the play begins?

8.      Is this an effective opening?

         How does it engage the audience's attention?

# General Vision and Viewpoint

The shadowy, dark setting creates a dark and troubled atmosphere.

Rosa has come to discover something of her birth mother, her reason for being here is personal and emotional.

Rosa's discovery of the baby picture is moving. The inscription reads, "My baby Rosa. My beautiful baby." There is a sense that Rosa's mother loved and wanted her, but lost her, adding a sense of loss and regret to the atmosphere.

The ledger states who signed these women in and and records the details of their babies. The fact that so many were signed in by their parents is saddening. It suggests a cold, cruel world, where so many could sign away their daughter's life like this.

The details of the stillborn babies adds a further note of sadness here, adding to the feeling that this is a place and story of sadness and suffering.

It is bleak and saddening to consider that women were locked up, and denied their freedom, because they were pregnant and unmarried. This adds to the dark outlook as the play begins.

1.      Why has Rosa come to the convent-laundry?

         How does this make you feel?

2.    What details does Rosa discover about Brigit?
      What other details does the ledger reveal?
      How does this information make you feel?

3.    In this world, young women were sent away for being
      pregnant, signed in to institutions by their own parents.
      Is this a positive or negative comment on life in your
      view?
      How do you feel about a world where this happens?

4.    How do you feel, viewing/reading this scene?
      What stands out for you as being particularly positive or
      negative?

5.    Is there darkness in this scene?
      Explain your point of view.

# Relationships

Rosa has come to the laundry to learn about her birth mother. Her
statement, "I had to come!" shows what this connection means to her.

Rosa is adopted and does not know the woman who gave birth to her.

This separation of mother and baby is a feature of relationships in this
text, leading to sadness and frustration amongst these women who are
prevented from knowing their children.

Many of the penitent women were signed in to the laundry by their
parents. This shows the power their parents had over them, that they could
sign away all freedom. It also suggests a coldness, that they could treat their
daughters this way, rather than loving and supporting them.

1. Why has Rosa come to the laundry?
   What does this tell you about her attitude to her birth mother?

2. What does Rosa discover on the back of the baby photo?
   What does this suggest?

3. Many of the penitent women were signed over to the laundry by their parents.
   Does this surprise you?
   Why did they sign their daughters in like this?
   What does this tell you about family relationships in this text?

# Hero, Heroine, Villain

### *Brigit*

We learn little of Brigit Murphy in this opening scene, except that she was a penitent woman, incarcerated in the laundry, and that she had a daughter, Rosa, who was adopted and did not know her.

1. What do you learn about Brigit Murphy in this scene?

# Act 1, Scene 2 - Morning Call

Sister Virginia completes the morning call with lighted candle and handbell.

## Cultural Context/Social Setting

The appearance of the nun and the chanting tells us that this is a place run by a religious order. This is an insight into the morning routine of the nuns, in their lives of prayer. We see the importance of routine, order and obedience in the morning call.

## Literary Genre

The action of the story has moved back in time to 1963. The audience will now bear witness to the lives of these penitent women at this time. Note the impact of the darkness, the lighted candle and the ringing bell. These atmospheric details add to the darkness and shadowiness on stage and create a sense of foreboding and curiosity about what is to come.

# Act 1, Scene 3 - Cathy's Birthday

Cathy is returned to the laundry after a failed escape attempt. The women celebrate her birthday.

## Cultural Context/Social Setting

The women are incarcerated in this laundry where they work washing the clergy's linen.

The women pretend to work as Mother Victoria arrives and Nellie-Nora hides her cigarette. Mother Victoria is in charge, the women's behaviour acknowledges her authority. Mother Victoria inspects their work, cleaning "His Lordship's" clothes and shoes. The term "His Lordship" shows how the Bishop is respected and revered.

Their work is part of the women's incarceration, with Mother Victoria acting as their overseer.

Brigit's mocking of the Bishop shows how these women are treated, "Gawd bless you, my scrubbers!...Stand up straight all of you!" They are to clean and scrub, and obediently follow the rules of the laundry. There is an expectation here that the Bishop would speak down to these women and tell them what to do. This shows us how this society works, the Bishop is powerful and influential, the women in the laundry are "scrubbers" who are used to being told how to behave.

Cathy's failed escape attempt shows that these women are prisoners, kept against their will in a Church run institution. The control and power of the Church is clear.

The children who see Cathy outside point and laugh at her, and call her names. This tells us how these women are looked down on and disrespected in their society.

Cathy says Mother Victoria gave her the "usual sermon" on her return and rubs her head, suggesting that she has been beaten. This shows how these women are treated by the nuns that run the laundry.

Mother Victoria tells Sister Virginia not to hand out letters to the women until tea-break. These women are of little importance to Mother Victoria, her priority is the work they must do.

These letters are a link to the outside world for the women. Cathy receives a card from her twins, showing that they know who and where she is. Cathy wonders if she will ever be a mother to them, prevented from this by her imprisonment in the laundry.

Mandy is excited at the prospect of Elvis' visit, reminding us of the 1960s setting.

The harsh treatment these women have received because of their pregnancies is seen here. Brigit calls love a trick, Mandy says her boyfriend, Richard, never spoke to her again after she told him about the baby. She only saw him once, in the distance, before being brought to the laundry. Her words make clear the treatment of women in this society, where they are sent away and locked up for the crime of being pregnant and unmarried.

It is important to note how easily Richard dealt with Mandy's pregnancy, never speaking to her before she was sent away, while he continues to enjoy life in the outside world. This is a world of double standards, where women are judged and condemned by a controlling, religious society, and men hypocritically escape the rules applied to women. Richard fathered Mandy's child and will suffer no ill consequence, while she is incarcerated and forgotten.

These women have been let down by the men they were involved with, and treated as expendable, locked away in the laundry to suffer their shame, while the men can continue with their lives. This is a sexist, unfair, unjust society, where women suffer society's judgements.

1.  "Aahk! The window's too high up, Mandy!"
    What do the women's efforts with the mirror and
    window tell you about their situation?

2.  How do the women react as Mother Victoria approaches?
    What does this tell you?

3.  How does Mother Victoria speak to the women?
    What does this tell you about this place?

4.  Nellie-Nora says, "But he's a Prince of the Church, Brigit!
    Mother Victoria told me!", when Brigit criticises the
    Bishop.
    What do Nellie-Nora's words reveal to you about this
    world?

5.  What has Cathy tried to do?
    What does this tell you about this place?

6.  What did the children do when they saw Cathy?
    What does this tell you about the society of this world?

7.  How was Cathy treated when she was returned to the
    laundry?
    What does this tell you about this world?

8.  "Give these letters out at tea-break, Sister! Not until tea-
    break! His Lordship's linens first!"
    What do Mother Victoria's words reveal to you about this
    place?

9.   What do the letters the women receive tell you about the world of the play?
     Be specific in your answer.

10.  What does Cathy's "party" tell you about this place?
     What insight does it give you into the women's world?

11.  What does the food the women imagine tell you about their usual diet?

12.  "Read my cup Nellie-Nora!"
     What is going on here?
     What does it show you about this world?

13.  "...when I told him about the baby, he never spoke to me again! Ever!"
     What do Mandy's words about her relationship with Richard tell you about this world?

14.  Why, do you think, did Richard never speak to Mandy again?

15.  What do the mannikin, the ringing convent bell and the women's conversation tell you about the role of the Church in their lives?

16.  What sort of place is this?
     What sort of life do the women have, based on what you have read/seen so far?
     What sort of life do the nuns have?
     Include examples to support your view.

17.     Is the Ireland of the play very different to modern day
        Ireland, based on what you have seen/read so far?
        Give reasons for your answer.

# Literary Genre

The scene opens with the women singing "Heartbreak Hotel", an Elvis
Presley number that places the action in the 1960s. The lyrics help to tell the
story here, as the women sing of being left by a lover, and finding this lonely
place to live.

It is clear that they are prisoners, searching for a glimpse of the world
outside. This idea of captivity, and the desire to escape, runs through this
scene.

As Mother Victoria approaches, the women rush to pretend to work.
Her position of authority and power is clear in the way they respond to her
arrival. Mother Victoria inspects a surplice. The roles of the women are seen
in their actions, the women work while the nun inspects.

When Mother Victoria leaves, Brigit is annoyed by the Bishop's luxury,
versus the women's situation. She dresses as him, making fun of him. This
pretence is the first of many flights of fancy, where the women imagine their
lives differently. When Brigit pretends to give gifts to the women, she shows
the audience all that they lack, as well as providing a moment of humour.

The mood changes when Mother Victoria brings in a tearful Cathy,
and demands that the women get to work. Cathy's failed escape attempt
demonstrates that the women are captives, deeply unhappy with their
imprisonment.

The letters the women read reminds us that they have lives outside the
laundry that they cannot participate in.

Mandy says Elvis is coming to visit, and later suggests pretending they are
in Paris, at a huge party for Cathy. Her fantasies contrast sharply with her

reality, there is a gulf between her imagined and real life.

Nellie-Nora's concern when she reads Cathy's tea-leaves raises audience interest and adds tension. We wonder what Nellie-Nora has seen to cause her distress, and how matters will play out. There is a sense of foreboding and danger to come.

Mandy's words about her boyfriend not speaking to her again when he learned of her pregnancy reinforces the audience's impression of injustice in these women's lives. The unfairness of their imprisonment is clear, it is their world that is punishing them for being pregnant and unmarried.

The women looking at photographs as the scene ends is sad and touching, showing the audience what they have lost.

The scene ends with machine sounds starting up, and lights lowering to create a sense of passing time, an effective technique that appeals to the senses.

This scene creates a sense of what life in the laundry is like. The women are portrayed as real and vulnerable, something that strikes an emotional chord with the audience.

1.   What is the effect of the women pulling down the drapes as the scene begins?

2.   What is the significance of the Bishop's soutane and surplice onstage?

3.   Why do the women sing "Heartbreak Hotel" as the scene begins?
     What is being communicated to the audience?

4.   What do the women think of Mother Victoria?
     Include a quotation in your answer.
     What does this add to the story?

5. What does Brigit pretending to be the Bishop add to the scene?

    Is this a funny moment?

    Explain your point of view.

6. What are your first impressions of Brigit's character and her situation?

    Use examples to support your view.

7. What does Brigit pretending to be the Bishop tell you about her?

8. What does Cathy's failed escape attempt add to the story?

9. How does the playwright make it clear to the audience that these women are prisoners?

    What is the effect of this on the audience?

10. What does the women receiving letters tell you about their lives?

11. What do Mandy's flights of fancy about Elvis and Paris add to the scene?

12. What changes the mood from the women's happy make-believe?

    Why does the playwright change the mood like this?

13. Nellie-Nora is distressed by what she sees in Cathy's tea-leaves.

    What does this add to the story?

14.    What does Mandy's story about Richard add to your sense
       of the setting?

15.    Look again at the stage directions as this scene ends.
       What is being communicated to the audience?
       Do you like this way of telling the story?
       Give reasons for your answer.

# General Vision and Viewpoint

The opening fragment from "Heartbreak Hotel" gives an insight into the
women's isolated, rejected state, cast aside into the laundry.

They are cheerful, hoping for a glimpse of a man outside, but their
unhappy lot is clear, "Back to penance!".

Mother Victoria's presence makes the women's position clear, they work
for the Church that controls their lives.

Brigit feels outrage that the Bishop should experience sunshine and wine
in Rome, while they live in the laundry. She rails against the system that
oppresses her, angered and frustrated by her incarceration. Brigit dresses as
the Bishop to mock him, but she is also mocking their lives. When Brigit
dresses up, Nellie-Nora warns her to be careful, showing the fear and tight
control the women live under. However, despite the fear and control, the
women have fun, laughing together. Their lives are not empty of joy and
friendship, a positive aspect in this bleak world.

Mother Victoria represents the power that holds the women captive
and dictates their lives. She demands that the women get to work. With
her is Cathy, who has just made a failed attempt to escape. She is however,
determined to try again, "I'll keep trying! I'm getting out!"

Cathy's escape attempt shows how she is resisting her imprisonment.
Mandy remarks, "you didn't try it again?", telling us that Cathy keeps trying

to be free, but is foiled each time. There is a sense of hopelessness in the way Cathy cannot escape from this place, "I fought. I bit them. I screamed. - But they brought me back."

Mother Victoria directs Sister Virginia not to give the women their letters until tea-break, another reminder that they are not free, but wards of the Church.

Cathy receives a birthday card from her children and wonders if she will ever be a mother to them. Her outlook is bleak as her future holds little hope of being with her children, something she wants desperately.

Mandy's excitement that Elvis will visit shows how empty her life is. She invests hope in this fantasy, but is sure to be disappointed, another dark aspect to the scene's outlook.

The other women join in imagining a party in Paris. They each participate in this momentary escape from their lives, and try to make each other happy through make-believe and pretence.

Nellie-Nora reads Cathy's tea-leaves and is distressed by what she sees, an ominous pointer towards what lies ahead for her. There is a sense of inescapable unhappiness and relentless oppression in these women's lives as they continue to be deprived of freedom and family.

Brigit calls love a trick, and Mandy recounts how her boyfriend never spoke to her again after she told him she was pregnant. This adds to the sense that life has been cruel to these women who have been deceived by the promise of love.

As the scene ends, the women look at photographs, reminding us of what they have lost, adding to the sense of unfairness in their lives.

1.      How does the Elvis song, "Heartbreak Hotel", contribute to the mood here?
        What does it tell you about these women's lives?

2.     "Sure I must have broken a lorry-load of mirrors to end up in this saltmine!"
   How does Nellie-Nora view her situation?

3.     "Rome! Sunshine! Wine! And look at us! That rip Victoria! God, how I hate her!"
   What insight do Brigit's words give you into how she feels about her life?
   How does this make you feel?

4.     As Brigit dresses as the Bishop, Nellie-Nora tells her to be careful.
   What does this tell you about Nellie-Nora's outlook?

5.     What does Cathy's escape attempt tell you about her life?
   How does this make you feel?

6.     "But I'm getting out! I'll keep trying! I'm getting out!"
   What do Cathy's words suggest about the human spirit?

7.     "It's alright Sister! If I got a letter now, I'd die of shock!"
   How do Nellie-Nora's words make you feel?
   What do they tell you about her life?

8.     Cathy receives a card from her children.
   Does this card add a positive or negative note to the scene?

9.     The women imagine they are at a party in Paris.
   Is this a happy moment?
   Explain your point of view.

10.     "Close your eyes and pretend! It'll be true if you pretend!"
        What does the women's pretence tell you about their
        lives?
        Is this a happy or saddening idea?

11.     "Love's a trick!"
        Explain Brigit's outlook here.
        What makes her feel this way?

12.     What does Richard's treatment of Mandy suggest about
        life?
        How does it make you feel?

13.     What sort of lives do the penitent women lead?
        How does this make you feel?
        What does this suggest about life?

14.     Do the women have reason to be hopeful about their
        futures?
        Is this an uplifting or upsetting outlook?
        Explain your point of view.

# Relationships

The women are friendly and comfortable together, chatting to Mandy about
the man she is looking out for.

Their behaviour changes as Mother Victoria approaches, and they
pretend to work. Mother Victoria speaks down to the women and orders
them about, concerned with His Lordship's clean shoes and linen. She is the
authority here, and the work of the laundry, rather than the welfare of the

women, is her concern.

Brigit's outburst when Mother Victoria leaves shows how much she resents her, "Some day I'll put her through the washing machines!"

The women have fun when Brigit pretends to be the Bishop, enjoying the silly pretence.

Mother Victoria brings in Cathy in tears. She has been caught moments after escaping from the convent-laundry. Cathy rubs her head, indicating that she has been beaten. This shows how the women are treated.

The women ask Cathy what happened and listen to her tale, a cohesive group.

Mother Victoria tells Sister Virginia not to give the women their letters until tea-break, showing her power and authority over them.

However, Sister Virginia finds it difficult to keep the women's letters from them. Mandy and Nellie-Nora plead with her to hand them out, but she reluctantly resists, conforming to her authoritative role. While Sister Virginia feels more warmly towards the women than her superior does, she is a part of the system that oppresses them.

The women receiving letters gives an insight into their relationships with those outside the laundry. Nellie-Nora never receives a letter, suggesting total separation from her life outside. Cathy receives a birthday card from her twins, and wonders if she will ever be a mother to them, something she clearly wants to be, but cannot because of her circumstances. We see how relationships are compromised and affected by the women's imprisonment in the laundry.

Nellie-Nora suggests a party for Cathy, and each of the women gives her a small gift, showing the strength and significance of their friendships. They try to celebrate Cathy's birthday despite their circumstances.

Nellie-Nora tells the women good things are in store for them after reading their tea leaves, even though Cathy's cup causes her distress. Nellie-Nora tries to make them happy, telling them what they want to hear.

All that Brigit wants is to be told she will find her baby, showing how much she cares about her lost child.

Mandy remembers how Richard, her boyfriend, did not speak to her again after learning that she was pregnant. This is a cold, cruel way to treat her, especially as he is her baby's father. It is however, worth considering whether his world has left him ill-equipped to deal with Mandy's predicament. In any case, he appears unfeeling and selfish, while Mandy found herself sent away, pregnant and alone.

1. How do the women treat one another?
   Are they friends, do you think?
   Give reasons for your answer.

2. How do the women act towards Mother Victoria?
   What is her relationship to the women?

3. How does Brigit feel about Mother Victoria?
   What makes her feel this way?

4. How do the women react when Sister Virginia arrives?
   Do they view her as the same as Mother Victoria?
   Give a reason for your answer.

5. What is the relationship between Sister Virginia and Mother Victoria?

6. Why is Cathy crying and rubbing her head when she arrives?
   What does this tell you about how Mother Victoria treats the women?

7. Is Sister Virginia good at being in charge of the women?
   Give a reason for your answer.

8. Does Cathy care about her children?

   Do they care about her?

   What is stopping Cathy from being a mother to them?

   How does this make you feel?

9. Is Cathy's "party" a good birthday party?

   What does it show you about the women's friendships?

10. "Elvis drops in! Sees our Mandy in her long lacy dress and falls madly in love with her!"

    How do the women treat one another?

    Use examples to support your view.

11. What does Nellie-Nora tell Cathy and Mandy after reading their tea-leaves?

    How does she treat them here?

12. How does Brigit feel about her lost child?

    What does this add to the theme of relationships?

13. How did Richard respond when Mandy told him about the baby?

    Did he care about her, in your view?

    What does Mandy's story about Richard add to the theme of relationships?

14. Does Mother Victoria respect the women in her care, in your opinion?

    Give reasons for your answer.

15. What stands out for you about the relationships in the play so far?

16.     Are relationships mostly positive or negative?
        Use examples to support your view.

# Hero, Heroine, Villain

*Brigit*

This scene gives an insight into how the women spend their time working in the laundry and how they are treated by the nuns.

Brigit is brave and defiant when she acts the part of the Bishop, "So, Brigit here will be Prince of the Church too!" She shows spirit and humour here, generously giving the women imaginary gifts.

Brigit joins in at Cathy's party, giving her love-hearts for her birthday and imagining Elvis at the pretend party in Paris.

Brigit is a strong-willed individual, who knows her own mind. She has no interest in having her tea-leaves read. She says, "Just tell me, that I'll find my baby!" Her determination to find her daughter is clear.

1.      What does Brigit pretending to be the Bishop tell you
        about her character?

2.      How does Brigit treat the other women?
        What does this tell you about her character?

3.      How does Brigit feel about Mother Victoria?
        What does this tell you about Brigit and her life in the
        laundry?

4.      "Elvis drops in! Sees our Mandy in her long lacy dress and
        falls madly in love with her!"

Is Brigit a good friend?

Fully explain your point of view.

5.       Why doesn't Brigit bother with the tea-leaves?

What does this tell you about her?

6.       What are your first impressions of Brigit?

What sort of person is she?

7.       Does Brigit have a hard life?

How would you feel, in her position?

# Act 1, Scene 4 - True Love

Juliet, a seventeen year old from the orphanage, joins the women in this scene. She fears the world outside, particularly men.

## Cultural Context/Social Setting

Juliet joins the women in the laundry. She is seventeen and has lived her life in the orphanage, a daughter of one of the women in the laundry. She has spent her life isolated from the world, denied a family because her mother was unmarried and sent to the laundry.

Sister Virginia encourages Juliet to think of life outside, but Juliet is fearful of men in the outside world. She recounts being attacked by Mick the vegetable man, who would have sexually assaulted her if he had not been interrupted. Juliet, an orphan girl, daughter of a fallen woman, is an easy target, of little consequence in this world. Mother Joachim does not believe that Juliet did not lead her attacker on, showing the view that women are sinful.

Sister Virginia and Juliet speak of the priesthood. It is a popular, well-respected vocation in this religious world.

Brigit asks Sister Virginia for the keys, wanting to go and see the father of her baby before he gets married. Sister Virginia cannot release her, as she is not in charge. There is a strict system of authority in place here, one which the young novice obeys.

Juliet asks about her mother. She was not allowed to see her before her death, showing the unfeeling rules in place here.

Brigit says Cathy was 'left in the lurch' by the twins' father, who abandoned her. Here it seems, women are disposable. Men retain their freedom and are free to live their lives, while pregnant women are sent to the laundry.

Mother Victoria tells Sister Virginia she has a visitor that she may see for ten minutes. Even Sister Virginia has little freedom.

Mother Victoria prays while the women work before turning her attention to the laundry, wanting to make sure His Lordship is looked after. The Bishop does not need to be present for his importance to be felt.

1. Juliet is seventeen, and from the orphanage.
   Does this tell you anything about this world?

2. How does Juliet view men?

3. What did Mick the vegetable man do to Juliet?
   What made him think he could do this?
   What does this tell you about how society views the children of the fallen women?

4. Mother Joachim would not believe that Juliet had not led Mick on.
   What does this tell you about how Mother Joachim views Juliet?
   Why does she view her this way?

5. Juliet is afraid of the outside world.
   What has made her this way?
   What insight does this give you into this place?

6. "Look Sister! More shirts from the seminary!"
   What do you notice about all of the work the women do?

7. "Nearly every mother west of the Shannon has a son studying for the priesthood."

Is this a religious world?

Explain your view.

What is the impact of religion in this world?

Use examples to support your ideas.

8.     What is stopping Sister Virginia from releasing Brigit?

What does this tell you about this world?

9.     "Bloody nuns! They don't give a damn!"

Do you agree with Brigit here?

Do the nuns care about the women?

Explain your view.

10.     Brigit says her uncle is an Archbishop.

If this is true, why hasn't he helped her?

11.     Brigit says that John-Joe, her baby's father, does not know about his daughter.

Does this surprise you in this world?

12.     The father of Cathy's twins "left her in the lurch".

What does this expression mean?

Did Cathy's boyfriend have a choice?

What else could he have done?

Who has the freedom to choose here?

Do the women have a say in what becomes of them?

13.     Why does Juliet admire Audrey Hepburn?

What does this tell you about how society sees and values women?

Is this different to or similar to today's society?

Support your viewpoint with examples.

14. "I'll give you ten minutes."
    What does Sister Virginia receiving a visitor show you
    about this world?

15. "Custody of the eyes, Sister!"
    What does this mean?
    What does it tell you about how women are seen in this
    world?

16. How does Mother Victoria spend her time with the
    women?
    What insight does this give you into this world?

17. How does Mother Victoria react to Brigit's singing?
    What does this tell you about this place?

18. "Tablecloths for the crimson gold dining-room"
    How does Mother Victoria view His Lordship?

19. Do the women matter to Mother Victoria?
    How do you know?

20. What sort of lives do the penitent women lead?
    Why is this the case?

21. How do men treat women in this world?
    What does this tell you about this culture?

22. What is life like for members of the Church?
    Include specific examples in your answer.

# Literary Genre

Juliet is from the orphanage. Her arrival makes very real the fate of the women's babies. She knows Cathy's daughters, adding to the audience's understanding of the sadness of their separation.

Juliet's fear of men and the world outside demonstrates how controlled and contained she is, adding to the themes of confinement and wrongful imprisonment.

The women explain aspects of their lives and backstories to Juliet in this scene, giving the audience an opportunity to learn more about them.

Brigit wants to get out to see John-Joe, her baby's father, who is getting married next week. Her frustration adds conflict and tension, and reinforces the audience's understanding of her lack of freedom.

Cathy has an attack of coughing, holding her head in pain before leaving in search of medicine. Nellie-Nora explains that Cathy is worn out and heart-broken. Her physical condition conveys this to the audience, we can visibly see the toll her heart-break has taken on her.

Like Mandy and her pictures of Elvis, Juliet has pictures of Audrey Hepburn, aspiring to be as thin as her. Once again, the playwright stresses the need for escape and fantasy in these women's lives. They collect these pictures for a momentary release from their lives as they imagine something else.

Mother Victoria arrives, beads and keys rattling, an audible reminder of the Church and its power.

Brigit sings while Mother Victoria prays, to the nun's annoyance. Here we see these characters clash, a brewing tension.

Brigit jokes that Nellie-Nora knits underwear for His Lordship. Brigit's lively spirit is clearly seen, especially when she mimics Mother Victoria. This mockery is a moment of brief relief, while her resistance to the nun's authority raises her in our estimation. The audience is invested in these women's lives, we want to see whether they can escape their imprisonment, if such a thing is possible.

Cathy's song of love, and Brigit's dismissal of the idea of love forever true reminds the audience of how these women's relationships with men have failed them, how a belief in love has yet to prove true.

Mother Victoria's wordless inspection of the women demonstrates that she is their warden, ensuring their confinement.

The effect of the lights lowering, women freezing, and the machine sounds as the scene ends is compelling. This creates the effect of this scene being a frozen snapshot, linking to the next scene. Thus, these dislocated fragments are linked together, a chain of moments in the narrative of these women's lives.

1.    How do the women react to Juliet's arrival?

2.    What is the effect of having the women work during this scene?

3.    Sister Virginia asks Juliet about living outside and speaks positively of men.
      What is she doing here?
      What does this tell you about Sister Virginia's character?
      What are your impressions of her so far?

4.    What does Juliet's tale of Mick the vegetable man add to this scene?
      What does this incident make clear to the audience?

5.    Why does Brigit want the keys?
      What does this add to the scene?

6.    "He doesn't know about Rosa!"
      What is the effect on the audience of hearing Rosa
      mentioned?

7.    What does Cathy's coughing and her physical pain signal
      to the audience?
      Is this an effective way of communicating this idea?
      Explain your view.

8.    What do the women's 'snaps' communicate to the
      audience?

9.    The stage directions state that Mother Victoria's beads
      and keys are rattling.
      What is the significance of her beads and keys?

10.   What does Sister Virginia do before she goes to meet her
      visitor?
      What does this tell us?

11.   Is Brigit afraid of Mother Victoria?
      How do you know?
      How does this affect your view of Brigit's character?

12.   How do Cathy's singing and Brigit's final words add to
      this scene?

13.   What is the effect of Mother Victoria wordlessly
      inspecting the women as the scene ends?

14.   How is a sense of imprisonment created in this scene?

15. Where have you noticed symbolism so far in the play?
What does this add to the storytelling?

# General Vision and Viewpoint

Juliet is seventeen and from the orphanage. It is sad to think that she has lived her whole young life in an institution, without a family, while her mother has led a similar life of loss and separation in the laundry.

Juliet has no wish to leave the laundry, wanting to stay in the place her mother lived until her death. She is afraid of the outside world, and of men in particular. Juliet describes being assaulted by the vegetable man, who threatened to kill her if she moved, before Old Mother Benedict arrived on the scene.

It is sad that Juliet has been raised to fear men, and also that her fears have been well-founded. It paints a bleak, hopeless view of life, where a seventeen year old should wish to shut herself away from the world because of the threat of sexual violence. Juliet's outlook is fearful, which adds to the text's bleak outlook.

Mother Joachim's belief that Juliet led Mick on, that she was somehow complicit in this unwanted attack, further darkens the outlook. This adds to the grim, disheartening view of life in the text, where a sexual predator is automatically in the right, and an innocent teenage girl is not believed.

Sister Virginia encourages Juliet to see life outside the laundry and asks Cathy to see that she eats. The novice's care and concern is a positive in this dark and trying world.

Brigit is frustrated and angry that she cannot go to see her baby's father before he marries. She is a prisoner, unable to affect the direction of her life.

Brigit's bitterness and vexation is clear as she curses the nuns who do not give a damn about her.

Juliet asks Cathy about her mother. She was not allowed to see her before her death. There is sadness in Juliet's loss, and in how the laundry authorities stopped her from seeing her mother like this.

Cathy, in pain and feeling unwell, goes for aspirin. Nellie-Nora says Cathy is heartbroken, with Brigit adding that she never speaks of the man who fathered her twins and left her in the lurch. The heartbreak and misery Cathy suffers is obvious, a sad aspect of her life.

Mother Victoria prays among the women, asking them to do the same, which Brigit resists. Even religion is imposed on these women, they have nothing of their own choosing in their lives.

1.      Juliet is seventeen, and from the orphanage.
   What is her life like?
   How does this make you feel?

2.      How does Cathy respond to hearing news of her daughters?
   How does this make you feel?
   How does Cathy's situation make you feel about life?

3.      "My Mammy lived here until she died. I want to stay in here!"
   What is Juliet's attitude to the outside world?
   What has made her feel this way?
   Is this saddening or heartening?

4.      What did Mick, the vegetable man, do to Juliet?
   How does this make you feel?

5.      Mother Joachim would not believe that Juliet didn't lead Mick on.

How does this make you feel?

What does this suggest about life?

6.    Sister Virginia encourages Juliet to see the world outside the laundry.

Does this add a note of hope to the scene?

Explain your point of view.

7.    "Bloody nuns! They don't give a damn!"

How is Brigit feeling?

How does her situation make you feel?

What does this add to the view of life the playwright offers?

8.    Juliet was not allowed to see her mother before she died.

What does this add to the view of life presented in the play?

9.    In this scene the playwright highlights a number of things the penitent women are missing in their lives.

What are they missing out on?

What sort of picture does this paint of their lives?

10.    What is wrong with Cathy, according to Nellie-Nora and Brigit?

What does this add to the mood?

11.    How did the father of Cathy's twins treat her?

What does this suggest about life?

How does this make you feel?

12.     "Is His Lordship's linen ready, Brigit?"
        How does Mother Victoria view these women?
        How does this make you feel?

13.     What is Brigit's view of love, based on this scene?
        What does this suggest about her life?
        How does this make you feel?

14.     How do the women treat one another in the laundry?
        What does this add to the view of life the play offers?

15.     Is Brigit a figure of resistance?
        How does this affect the general vision and viewpoint?

16.     Is resistance futile for these women?
        How does this affect the general vision and viewpoint?

17.     Are there bright moments in this scene?
        Explain your view.

18.     How do you feel, experiencing this story?
        Use examples to support your ideas.

# Relationships

When Cathy hears Juliet is from the orphanage, her first questions are of her twins, Michele and Emily. She is eager to learn whatever she can about them, and is upset because she is missing them growing up. As with Rosa and Brigit, loss, separation and upset characterise this relationship.

Brigit asks Sister Virginia to give her the keys. Sister Virginia is regretful that she cannot help her, saying that she is not in charge. Like the women,

Sister Virginia, a novice, cannot break the rules.

Brigit wants to go to see John-Joe, her baby's father, before he marries next week. She wants to tell him about his daughter. Brigit obviously cares about him, and feels he has a right to know about his child.

Juliet asks Cathy about her mother. Like so many of the play's characters, Juliet and her mother were separated and denied a close relationship. Juliet was not allowed to see her mother when she had a heart attack, which shows the power the laundry's authorities wield over the women.

Cathy tells Juliet that they will look after her, showing the caring solidarity of these women.

Brigit tells Juliet that Cathy never speaks of the "rotten bastard" who left her in the lurch. Cathy, it seems, was let down and abandoned by her babies' father, another case of a woman being discarded by her boyfriend.

Mother Victoria arrives, a symbol of authority in the women's lives, and prays while they work. Her concern is the laundry, and His Lordship's linen in particular. These women are her unpaid workforce, the satisfactory completion of their work is all she cares about.

The women themselves treat one another with understanding, doing their best to offer one another what limited support they can.

1.  How do the women greet Juliet?
    Are they welcoming?

2.  What does Cathy ask Juliet when she hears she is from the orphanage?
    What does this tell you?

3.  Is Sister Virginia kind to Juliet?
    Explain your view.

4.      Consider Juliet's story about Mick the vegetable man.
        What does it add to your understanding of how men treat
        women in this text?

5.      Brigit's uncle is an Archbishop.
        Why, do you think, hasn't he helped her?
        What does this suggest about family relationships in the
        text?

6.      Why does Brigit want to see John-Joe?
        What does this tell you about their relationship?

7.      Juliet asks Cathy about her mother.
        What does this tell you about how she feels about her?

8.      "They wouldn't let me see her!"
        How are the women treated by those in power?

9.      Brigit says that Cathy was 'left in the lurch'.
        What does this mean?
        What does it add to your understanding of relationships
        in this text?

10.     How does Mother Victoria speak to Sister Virginia when
        she tells her she has a visitor?
        What does this tell you about their relationship?

11.     How does Mother Victoria view the women?
        Use examples to support your ideas.

12.     Based on what you have seen/read so far, how do the
        penitent women treat one another?
        What characterises their relationships?

# Hero, Heroine, Villain

*Brigit*

Brigit wants to get out to see John-Joe, her baby's father, who is to be
married next week. He does not know about his daughter, Rosa, and Brigit
wants to tell him, feeling he has a right to know about his baby.

Brigit is frustrated and angry and curses the nuns and the Church, saying
they do not give a damn.

She calls the man who left Cathy in the lurch a rotten bastard, and says
women are fools for protecting men the way they do. She is a lively, spirited
character, who is not afraid to speak her mind or say what she feels.

When Mother Victoria suggests that they say the Rosary together, Brigit
objects, pointing out how many prayers they have already said. She is not
afraid to disagree with Mother Victoria.

While Mother Victoria prays, Brigit sings a song of lost love. She does
not show commitment to the Church or prayer.

Brigit jokes that Nellie-Nora is knitting "crimson combinations"
(underwear) for His Lordship, shocking Nellie-Nora. This shows Brigit's
humour and spirit, and the fact that she is not afraid of Mother Victoria.

1.      Why does Brigit want the keys?

2.      How does Brigit feel about John-Joe, do you think?
        Give a reason for your answer.

3.  "Bloody nuns! They don't give a damn!"
    How does Brigit feel about her life, do you think?

4.  Does Brigit have a lot of spirit?
    Use examples to support your view.

5.  How does Brigit respond when Mother Victoria says they
    will say the Rosary?

6.  What does Brigit do while Mother Victoria prays?
    What does this tell you about her?

7.  What joke does Brigit make about Nellie-Nora's knitting?
    What does this tell you about her?

# Act 1, Scene 5 - Credo Scene

Sister Virginia has a crisis of faith, grappling with the concerns she has over the treatment of the penitent women.

## Cultural Context/Social Setting

This scene makes clear that the Church is a significant force in this world, as Sister Virginia tries to pray amongst the voices of the suffering women. The convent-laundry is a place of religion and sorrow.

Mother Victoria's voice tells Sister Virginia that nobody else wants these women, showing how they have been rejected by society.

Her voice also reminds Sister Virginia of her vow of obedience. In this world, Sister Virginia is to obey the rule of the Church and do as she is told, not question those in power.

The voices of the women show that this is a place of suffering and confinement.

1.     "He descended into Hell"
       Is the laundry a sort of hell?
       Give reasons for your answer.

2.     Mother Victoria's voice tells Sister Virginia that no-one
       else wants these women.
       What do her words tell you about this society?

3.     "A vow of Obedience, Sister! Blind Obedience!"
       What do Mother Victoria's words tell you about Sister
       Virginia's place in this world?

What do her words tell you about the authority of the Church?

4.     Why is Sister Virginia disillusioned with the Church? What does this tell you about this world?

5.     What does this scene highlight about the Church?

6.     What does this scene highlight about the women's lives?

7.     What does this scene make clear to you about the convent-laundry?

# Literary Genre

This is a powerful, dramatic and moving scene, rich in symbolism. It is a moment of insight into Sister Virginia's thoughts, and the effect on the audience is jarring.

The chanting, stained glass window and sanctuary lamp are symbolic of the Church that Sister Virginia is struggling with.

Sister Virginia lying prostate and kneeling shows her vulnerability, as well as her submissive position in the Church. Lying in the shape of the cross conjures the idea of crucifixion, suffering and sacrifice.

Sister Virginia prays aloud, stating her belief in "God the Father Almighty..." However, her doubt and uncertainty are clear in the questioning tone of her voice. The audience is witnessing Sister Virginia having a crisis of faith, examining her belief. As she prays, the women's voices interrupt her, pleading for their babies and asking for help. This is a very effective technique, the audience hears the distressed voices of the women and understands how they prey on Sister Virginia's mind. The voice of Mother

Victoria is also heard, telling the novice that they care for these unwanted women.

These disembodied voices interrupting Sister Virginia at prayer are very dramatic, showing Sister Virginia's uncertainty and confusion, while simultaneously demonstrating that she cares about these women and dwells on their suffering.

This surreal display of Sister Virginia's torment is very engaging and arresting for the audience. Her inner conflict is perfectly realised, as is the ever-present authority of the Church in the words of Mother Victoria.

In her final prayer in this scene, Sister Virginia moves from questioning God, and her place in the Church, to imploring Him to help the penitent women. Her pleas for help are emotional, and show her distress very effectively.

1.	What does the playwright's use of light and darkness bring to this scene?

2.	What do the actions and gestures of Sister Virginia bring to this scene?

3.	Sister Virginia prays to God the Father Almighty.
	Does her belief sound steadfast to you?
	How are her doubts and concerns communicated to the audience?
	Is this effective storytelling?
	Explain your view.
	What is the effect of the women's voices interrupting Sister Virginia's prayer?

4.	What do these voices interrupting Sister Virginia's prayer tell you about her character?

5. "She's chokin' Sister!"
   What is the effect of hearing of the women's suffering in their own voices?

6. "Was crucified, died and was buried. He descended into Hell."
   What is the effect of the imagery here?

7. What impact does Mother Victoria's voice have on the scene?
   How does this add to the tension and contribute to the atmosphere?

8. Is Sister Virginia's closing speech moving?
   What makes it so?

9. Is this a dramatic scene?
   Give reasons for your answer.

10. Comment on the symbolism in this scene and what it adds to the story.

11. What, do you think, will Sister Virginia do as a result of this scene?

# General Vision and Viewpoint

In this scene, Sister Virginia has a crisis of conscience and faith. As she attempts to pray, the voices of the women and Mother Victoria crowd her thoughts, interrupting her.

This is a dark scene as Sister Virginia contemplates the treatment of the women at the hands of the Church, and tries to align this with her faith. Sister Virginia questions her part in the Church, disillusioned with the part she plays in the laundry.

Sister Virginia's empathy towards the women is obvious, she is clearly moved by their suffering and Mother Victoria's indifference.

This sense of indifference adds a hopeless note to the scene, the mother superior does not care about these women, it is unlikely that anything will change in their lives.

There is a sense of despair in Sister Virginia's closing speech, as she questions her part in the Church and pleads for God to help her and these women. She is very low and distressed, and gains no comfort from her prayer. This is a grim moment, highlighting how difficult these women's lives are.

Sister Virginia wonders at the toll this place will take on her, asking if she is being brain-washed. Her fears that her sense of self and integrity are being compromised is troubling, adding to the bleakness of this moment.

1. What is Sister Virginia struggling with in this scene?

2. "Was crucified, died and was buried. He descended into Hell."
   How does Sister Virginia's prayer affect the atmosphere?

3. "Mandy thought she could leave if she wasn't pregnant, so she performed an abortion on herself!"
   How does hearing of the women's suffering make you feel?

4. How does Sister Virginia feel about her part in the Church?

5.      Is there a sense of confusion or despair in this scene?
        Give reasons for your answer.

6.      What doubts and fears does Sister Virginia have?
        What do these doubts and fears reveal about her as a
        person?
        Is this a positive or negative aspect of her humanity?

7.      Is this a dark scene?
        Give reasons for your answer.

8.      Does Sister Virginia have a positive or negative outlook
        on her life in the Church?
        Explain your view.

9.      From what you have seen/read so far, is life fair for these
        characters?
        What does this suggest about the author's view of life?

# Relationships

In this scene, Sister Virginia's prayers are interrupted by the pleading voices
of the women, and the indifferent tone of Mother Victoria.

Sister Virginia cares about these women and their suffering and
treatment at the hands of the Church has shaken her faith. Sister Virginia
ends the scene praying for God to help her and these women. Her concern
and regard for the women is a positive aspect of the theme of relationships,
showing warmth, empathy and understanding.

1. "A kettle! Steam! Hurry, Sister! Hurry!"
   Do the penitent women rely on the nuns?

2. Does Sister Virginia care about the women in the laundry?
   What does this add to the theme of relationships?

3. Does Mother Victoria care about the women in the laundry?
   What does this add to the theme of relationships?

4. Are the women prisoners?
   Why do the nuns keep the women this way?

5. Does Sister Virginia have a good relationship with Mother Victoria?
   Explain your view.

# Hero, Heroine, Villain

*Sister Virginia*

This scene depicts Sister Virginia's inner crisis of faith as she prays while considering the suffering of the penitent women and Mother Victoria's indifference to their plight.

Sister Virginia cares about the women and is troubled by their treatment. She questions what she is doing and her involvement with the nuns, an examination of conscience that shows integrity and morality.

This scene ends with Sister Virginia begging God to help her and the women in her care. She cares about them, and knows they are being wronged by the Church.

1. What does this scene tell you about Sister Virginia's state of mind?

2. What is causing Sister Virginia to question her faith?

3. "You're supposed to be a Loving Father!"
   How does Sister Virginia feel about God?

4. "Am I being brain-washed?"
   How does Sister Virginia feel about her position in the Church?

5. How is Sister Virginia feeling as this scene ends?
   What does this tell you about Sister Virginia?

6. What sort of person is Sister Virginia, based on what you have seen/read so far?
   Include examples to support your ideas.

# Act 1, Scene 6 - Effigy

In this scene Brigit pours scorn on Mandy's talk of Elvis. Seeing that she has upset Mandy, Brigit then initiates a surreal make-believe wedding, where Mandy flies to Hollywood and marries Elvis Presley.

## Cultural Context/Social Setting

Some women work at wash-tubs with wash-boards, while others iron and mend. Theirs is a world of endless drudge work. A mannikin stands wearing a Bishop's soutane, a lifeless overseer. All of this laundry is the clergy's, all of this work is for them.

Mandy's letter to Elvis, and Juliet and Nellie-Nora's interest in it, shows an innocent, naive side to these women. They are like young girls, writing a letter to a sweetheart. Their innocence is at odds with the place they find themselves in.

Brigit reacts to Mandy's letter-writing, saying that Elvis would have nothing to do with her, knowing her address. Brigit understands completely how society views the women in the laundry, and that the world outside wants nothing to do with them.

After Brigit's outburst, she pretends to send Mandy to Hollywood to see Elvis, a trip that signifies glamour and luxury to the women. When Mandy is wed, Nellie-Nora says, "Have as many babies as you want now, Mandy!" Only as a married woman can she have children in this world.

> 1.     What do the props in this scene tell you about this world? Be specific in your answer.

2.      "Sister Virginia is not allowed to look at filmstars."
Why, do you think, is this the case?

3.      What does Mandy's letter to Elvis tell you about these women?

4.      "Saint Paul's Home for the women nobody wants!"
What does Brigit's outburst tell you about this world?
Why does nobody want these women?

5.      Why do the women pretend Mandy is off to Hollywood?
What does this tell you about their world?

6.      Is Mandy happy to be getting married?
What does this tell you about this society's values?

7.      What does this scene reveal to you about this world?
Include examples in your answer.

8.      What picture are you forming of life in the laundry?
How would you feel about living here?

# Literary Genre

The women are hard at work in the laundry. The mannikin dressed as a Bishop oversees all they do, an absent male presence, a visual reminder of the Church's authority.

Mandy continues to talk about Elvis, engaging in a fantasy world rather than her grim reality. Her excitement in writing her letter shows an innocent, childish side to these incarcerated women. She is as giddy as a young girl writing a letter to her sweetheart. Mandy's innocence, and that of Juliet and Nellie-Nora, is totally at odds with their surroundings. Brigit's scornful words, spoiling Mandy's dream, seem harsh, but her truth holds for the audience. Mandy's misplaced hope seems pitiful when Brigit states their reality, "Home for the unwanted. The outcasts!" The playwright cleverly balances a childish hope with their harsh reality, to make the audience realise the full reality of the women's trapped and lost lives.

Brigit's outburst and tussle with Mandy upsets her. This moment of conflict is tense and troubling. In this instant the women's awful reality is glaringly obvious, and one cannot escape the injustice and cruelty of their situation.

Brigit apologises immediately and begins a game where Mandy meets Elvis. Brigit's warmth is seen as she tries to make amends. The innocence of the women is seen in this game, this fun distraction from their grim lives. They revel in it, laughing and giggling, and involve themselves completely in dressing the mannikin.

The women's pretence may appear pathetic now, in the aftermath of Brigit's assertion of their rejected, hopeless state. The audience feels sorry for them and their childish games. It is pitiful that this is what they must do to be happy.

Throughout their pretence, Juliet is look-out. Her watchfulness keeps tension throughout the scene, and when she says someone is coming, we worry that the women will be caught. Even as they have fun and share laughter, anxiety brews in the audience, adding to the continued emotional force of the scene.

Just as this scene deepens our understanding of the women's plight, it also adds to our understanding of Sister Virginia's character. She does not interrupt the women's game, showing kindness and compassion towards them.

Ending on a lovesong is emotionally engaging. Singing of heartbreak and loss reminds the audience of all these women have already lost.

1.      Look carefully at the stage directions as this scene begins.
        What do each of the directions bring to the setting?
        What is the audience's attention being focused on?
        What stands out for you here?

2.      "But not Elvis! Remember he's mine! He belongs to me!"
        Mandy continues to speak constantly of Elvis.
        What is the effect of this on the story?
        What is the effect of this on the audience?

3.      Is Mandy naive and innocent to believe Elvis gets all her
        letters?
        Is this a light-hearted moment?

4.      What is the effect on the audience of Brigit's outburst?

5.      Is Brigit cruel to spoil Mandy's dream of Elvis?

6.      Brigit apologises and begins a game where Mandy meets
        Elvis.
        What does this reveal to you about Brigit's character?

7.      "Hop in, Mandy! Now's your chance! Off to Hollywood!"
        Does this pretence seem fun or foolish to you?
        How does it change the mood at this point?

8.      What is the effect of the Elvis game on the audience?
        Fully explain your point of view.

9.      Why does Nellie-Nora tell Juliet to watch the door?
        How does this impact on the scene?

10.   Is the juxtaposition of Brigit's outburst and Mandy's imaginary trip to Hollywood jarring?
      What is the effect of these moments side by side?
      What is the impact on the audience?

11.   "There's someone comin' down the corridor!"
      What is the effect on the audience of Juliet sounding the alarm?

12.   How do the women react to Mandy's wedding?
      Is this an exciting moment?
      How does it make you feel?

13.   What is the effect of the music as the scene ends?

14.   Do you find any aspect of this scene jarring, unsettling or upsetting?
      Explain your view.

15.   Is this scene emotional?
      Use examples to support your ideas.

# General Vision and Viewpoint

As the women work, Cathy has difficulty breathing. Nellie-Nora and Brigit encourage her to talk about her troubles. There is warmth and compassion in the support they offer her.

Nellie-Nora says they will all go to heaven when they die. Though Brigit scoffs at this comment, it must bring Nellie-Nora comfort, just as Mandy's Elvis fantasy brings comfort to her. These beliefs make their lives more bearable, they look forward to better times. The unlikelihood of Mandy ever meeting Elvis tinges her hope with sadness. As an audience, we realise this is false hope she clings to, a saddening fact.

Brigit crushes Mandy's dreams of Elvis, saying he would never want her, belonging as she does to "Saint Paul's Home for the women nobody wants!" Brigit's anger adds to the emotion of Mandy's tears. This is a dark, upsetting moment, as Brigit asserts what they all know to be true. Theirs is a dark, hopeless world, where they are forever unwanted.

Brigit, at Cathy and Nellie-Nora's urging, apologises and begins a new Elvis game for Mandy. She tries to make amends for upsetting Mandy, a kind gesture.

The pretence itself, that Mandy is meeting Elvis, may appear childish and pathetic. The women commit wholeheartedly to their make-believe, while Brigit's harsh words of truth, spoken only moments earlier, sit heavily with the audience. The gaity of this pretence clashes with their harsh, grim reality, and lack of hope for a better future.

The women participate fully in their fantasy, dressing the mannikin so Mandy can marry it. What may appear as a light-hearted, fun distraction, also serves as a reminder of all that these women's lives lack. They act out a wedding that will never happen, their pretence will be short-lived, their laughter fleeting, their bleak lives, permanent.

Even as we see the women's capacity for love and laughter, their imprisoned state and hopeless outlook is clear. There is a sense that they have been cheated out of their lives.

The pretend marriage of Mandy and Elvis, which brings her such delight, highlights that she will never get to marry. This charade is a mockery, a childish attempt to live their lives as they might have been. Their fun draws attention to all they will never have, their empty futures stretch before them, full of the drudgery of the laundry and little else.

On a positive note, Sister Virginia witnesses the pretend marriage, but does not interrupt, allowing the women to enjoy it. Her kindness shows the compassionate, understanding side of human nature.

1.  Are the women kind to Cathy as this scene begins?
    What does this suggest about life?

2.  Does her faith bring Nellie-Nora comfort?
    Does her faith bring Brigit comfort?
    How do their views add to the play's outlook?

3.  What does Mandy believe in, to bring her comfort?
    Do you feel happy, or sorry for her, because of this?
    Explain your view.
    How does this add to the general vision and viewpoint?

4.  "Home for the unwanted. The outcasts! Saint Paul's Home
    for the women nobody wants!"
    Does Brigit accurately describe the women's world?
    How does this make you feel?

5.  Brigit apologises after her outburst and begins a new
    Elvis game.
    Why does she do this?
    What does this tell you about human nature?

6.  Do the women enjoy their game?
    What does this suggest about human nature?

7.  What does the pretence of Mandy going to Hollywood
    and marrying Elvis make clear about these women's lives?
    Is this moment uplifting or depressing?
    Explain your view.

8.      What does this scene highlight about what the women lack?

What is the effect of this on the viewer?

9.      Is the wedding scene festive and celebratory?

Explain your view.

10.     Does this scene end on a happy note?

Explain your view.

11.     Is it sad, that these women have lost so much?

Do you feel sorry for them?

Explain your view.

12.     Are these women strong and resilient, or defeated by their lives?

How does this make you feel?

What does it suggest about life?

# Relationships

As the scene begins, Brigit and Nellie-Nora encourage Cathy to talk about her troubles, offering her support.

Juliet enjoys the fun of Mandy's letter to Elvis. Brigit erupts, destroying the idea of Elvis ever being with Mandy once he knows she is from the laundry. Her words are harsh and cutting.

Mandy and Brigit push each other, and Mandy falls crying to the floor. Here, we see how difficult these women's relationships can be, how the strain and frustration of their lives can impact negatively on their relationships with one another.

Brigit apologises immediately, encouraged to by Nellie-Nora and Cathy. She then initiates an elaborate pretence where Mandy is posted to Elvis to meet him. She is making amends for her harsh words, trying to make Mandy happy again, a positive gesture.

The women enjoy pretending that Mandy is going to Hollywood to meet Elvis, and they giggle and laugh together. This is a shared moment of fun and happiness, and they each add to the pretence to add to the enjoyment.

Sister Virginia arrives as Elvis and Mandy wed, but does not interfere or interrupt. Her actions show compassion and kindness towards the women, she does not want to spoil their happiness.

This scene draws attention to the lack of love and romance in the women's lives. Cut off from the world, they have to invent romance, and pretend it is possible, a saddening aspect of this theme.

1. The women see that Cathy is troubled.
   How do they treat her?
   What does this tell you about their friendships?

2. How does Brigit react to Mandy's letter to Elvis?
   Is Brigit being fair here?

3. Is Brigit annoyed with Mandy, or something else?
   Explain your view.

4. What makes Brigit apologise to Mandy straight away?
   What does this tell you about the women's relationships?

5. What makes Brigit make-believe that Mandy is going to see Elvis?
   What does this tell you about the women's relationships?

6. Why do the women join in this game?

7.     What does Mandy's pretend wedding to Elvis tell you about how these women treat each other?

8.     Sister Virginia arrives but does not interrupt the wedding.
What does this tell you about how she feels about the women?

9.     What makes the women's relationships with each other difficult?
Fully explain your point of view.

10.     Do the women have many positive relationships in their lives?
Use examples to support your view.

11.     Will Mandy ever get to wed in real life?
What does this add to the theme of relationships?

# Hero, Heroine, Villain

*Brigit*

Brigit tells Cathy to talk about her troubles and says she is better than this place. Her words show kindness and compassion.

Brigit scoffs at the idea that they will go to heaven when they die. She does not share Nellie-Nora's faith.

She jokes about Father Durcan's looks, showing humour and spirit.

When Mandy writes a letter to Elvis, Brigit cannot contain her scorn. She says Elvis would have nothing to do with Mandy, that they are the women no-one wants. She is harsh and unkind here, cruelly speaking the truth to Mandy and robbing her of the comfort of her fantasy. Clearly, Brigit is frustrated by her life in the laundry and reacts to this frustration, taking it out on those closest to her.

She apologises straight away to Mandy, and pretends that they will post Mandy to Elvis. This pretence lightens the mood and is a moment of brief fun for the women.

Brigit's flash of rage passes quickly. She commits to this elaborate pretence, dressing the mannikin and telling Mandy he wants to marry her, and acting as the Bishop officiating the wedding.

1.　How does Brigit treat Cathy as the scene begins?

2.　Is Brigit religious?

3.　"You'd be finished with him!"
　　How does Brigit treat Mandy over the letter-writing?
　　Is Brigit cruel here?

4.　What makes Brigit apologise straight away?

5.　"I've a great idea! We'll post Mandy off to Hollywood!"
　　What is Brigit doing here?

6.　Are you surprised that Brigit starts a make-believe scenario where Mandy meets Elvis?
　　Fully explain your point of view.

7.　Why, do you think, does Brigit commit to the elaborate pretence of Mandy's meeting with Elvis?

8.　What does this scene tell you about Brigit's life?

9. Is Brigit a likeable character?
   Explain your view.

10. What characteristics of Brigit's have you noticed so far?
    Are you building a positive or negative picture of her in
    your mind?
    Explain your view.

# Act 2, Scene 1 - Office 1

Sister Virginia visits Mother Victoria in her office and questions the way the women are treated.

## Cultural Context/Social Setting

Sister Virginia visits Mother Victoria in her office. Mother Victoria answers the phone to a priest, speaking of ledgers and cheques. Hers is a world of industry and business, she is effectively the warden and manager of the convent-laundry.

Mother Victoria gives Sister Virginia permission to sit, and to dispose of her chocolates. The authority and strict rules of the convent are apparent.

Sister Virginia says the women need their children, but Mother Victoria says they are weak and not to be trusted. She says no-one wants the women, showing how they have been rejected by society. Mother Victoria says the Church protects, feeds and clothes the women, believing that they are cared for by the Church.

Sister Virginia says the women need more. She is worried about Cathy in particular. Sister Virginia's concerns highlight that only the women's most basic needs are met, but the Church deems this satisfactory.

Mother Victoria is unmoved. She says the women are weak, sinful and treacherous, showing how they are viewed by society.

Mother Victoria blames Sister Virginia's lack of understanding on the fact that she has yet to take vows and so cannot understand God's way. The mysterious power of God is not to be questioned, it is Sister Virginia's youthful thinking that is at fault.

Mother Victoria mentions the mothers of some of the women in the laundry - they were born into this life of captivity and drudgery, their freedom lost because of the Church's belief that they are sinful.

Mother Victoria warns Sister Virginia to be careful when Brigit has bleach, showing her fear and distrust of the women.

Sister Virginia expresses doubts over the work of the laundry, calling the women drudges and bond-women, forced to perform menial labour. Mother Victoria tells her to submerge her doubts in the Rule of the Church, the Church's authority is the answer to everything in her view.

1.     What do the details of Mother Victoria's office tell you about what is important in her world?

2.     Do a lot of rules govern Sister Virginia?
Use examples from this scene in your answer.

3.     How does Mother Victoria view the penitent women?
Include quotation in your answer.

4.     "No one wants those women!"
Are Mother Victoria's words true?
What comment is she making on her society?

5.     "Cathy was hysterical! I had to slap her - "
What does Mother Victoria's treatment of Cathy reveal to you about this world?

6.     "I wanted to free the penitents - mothers of some of the women in the laundry now."
What is going on here?
What does this tell you about these women's lives?

7.  " this weakness to sins of the flesh stays in the blood for seven generations!"
    How does the Church view these women?

8.  "St Paul may have been afraid of women! Women tempt men! Remember the Garden! Eve started it all!"
    How does the Church view women in this world?
    Is this very different to how the Church views women today?

9.  What warning does Mother Victoria give Sister Virginia?
    What does this tell you about the laundry?

10. Is it possible to argue with the ways of the Church in this world?
    Give reasons for your answer.

11. Has life in the convent-laundry met Sister Virginia's expectations?
    What does this tell you about this world?

12. How does Mother Victoria handle Sister Virginia's doubts?
    What does this tell you about the Church and their world?

13. Does Mother Victoria have complete faith in the Church?
    Does this surprise you?

# Literary Genre

The props in the office are symbols, creating a sense of the importance of the Church and business to Mother Victoria, something reinforced by her phone conversation of ledgers and cheques.

Sister Virginia challenges Mother Victoria over the way the women are treated in the laundry. She shows bravery, confronting her superior like this. This dramatic scene is tense and exciting as Sister Virginia initiates this conflict.

This scene reveals the true nature of these characters. One is caring, brave and deeply concerned, while the other is callous, cold-hearted and prejudiced.

The playwright uses Mother Victoria to give voice to how the Church truly views the penitent women in its care. She calls them weak, sinful, and treacherous, revealing how the Church and society looks down on them.

Mother Victoria says no-one wants the women in the laundry, echoing Brigit's earlier words. This repetition stresses and reinforces how forsaken the women are.

Sister Virginia is an advocate for the women, challenging Mother Victoria and expressing all that they have lost at the hands of the Church.

Mother Victoria does not heed Sister Virginia's doubts, telling her to commit herself to the Church, rid herself of pride and obey the rule. It is frustrating to see Sister Virginia's brave challenge fail. The plain chant as the scene ends re-states the power and position of the Church. Sister Virginia's challenge has failed, and so the tension towards a resolution must continue.

1.      How do the props in Mother Victoria's office add to your sense of this place and her character?

2.   Is Sister Virginia brave to speak to Mother Victoria like this?
      What does this show you about Sister Virginia's character?

3.   Is this a conflict-rich scene?
      Explain your view.

4.   Is this an exciting scene?
      Explain your view.

5.   Does Mother Victoria effectively portray how the Church views the fallen women?
      Explain your view.

6.   What is the significance of the term "Eclipsed"?
      What does it mean?

7.   What makes this scene dramatic and emotionally powerful?
      Use examples and quotations in your answer.

8.   How do you feel about these characters as this scene ends?

9.   What is the effect of the plain chant as the scene ends?

10.  What is the effect of light and shadow in this scene?

11.  As an audience, did we need this scene?
      Explain your view.

# General Vision and Viewpoint

In Mother Victoria's office, Sister Virginia speaks up on the women's behalf, questioning the way they are locked away.

Mother Victoria reveals how she feels about the women: they are not to be trusted, they are weak and without control. Her judgement of these women is saddening and upsetting, showing the prejudice and intolerance of this world.

Sister Virginia stresses that these women need more in their lives, and better treatment, but Mother Victoria rejects her views, dismissing the novice as not yet understanding. Mother Victoria cites the weakness and sinfulness of the women, and warns Sister Virginia to be careful around them. Her prejudice and judgement adds to her coldness and lack of humanity. She views these women as lesser, unworthy and dangerous, all because they were pregnant without being married. Her words are disheartening, saddening and maddening, painting a dark worldview full of judgement and punishment.

Sister Virginia says if she were Brigit or Cathy, with her baby taken from her, she would tear down the walls with her nails. Her words show empathy and total understanding. Her emotion and compassion for the women is clear. Sister Virginia recognises the injustice served to these women, and is trying to do something about it, a positive attempt in this grim place. While there is daring and bravery in the novice's words, her frustration highlights how bleak life is for the women. They have been wronged, and can do nothing about it. Their freedom continues to be denied to them, a dark and harrowing reality.

Mother Victoria is unmoved by Sister Virginia's argument. She tells the novice to change herself and commit to the Church. There is nowhere for independent thinking in Mother Victoria's outlook, the Church must be obeyed. Hers is a rigid worldview, where the rule of the Church is supreme, and the lives of individuals matter little.

Sister Virginia tells her superior she will try to change, and leaves, unsuccessful in her attempt to get through to the woman, or change the women's lives. This is a dark moment where any hope of a better future for the incarcerated women looks impossible.

1. "But isn't our God a Loving Father, a Forgiving Father?" How do you feel when Sister Virginia challenges Mother Victoria over the treatment of the penitent women?

2. "Cathy was hysterical! I had to slap her - " How does Mother Victoria's treatment of Cathy make you feel?

3. Mother Victoria mentions the mothers of some of the current women in the laundry, showing they have been born and lived their lives here. What is your response to this? How does this make you feel?

4. "Women tempt men!" How does Mother Victoria's view of women colour her outlook? How does it affect her view of life? Is hers a positive or negative outlook?

5. "If I were Brigit or Cathy and my babies were taken from me, I'd tear down the walls with my nails!" What makes Sister Virginia feel this way? What does this add to the general vision and viewpoint?

Is there a sense of futility or hopelessness in her words?
Explain your point of view.

6.     Is Sister Virginia brave to speak up for the women to
       Mother Victoria?
       What does this tell you about human nature?

7.     "Do not question the system!"
       Describe Mother Victoria's worldview.

8.     Does Sister Virginia get through to Mother Victoria in
       this scene?
       What does this suggest about life?
       Will matters improve for the women?
       How does this make you feel?

9.     Does Sister Virginia give up at the end of the scene?
       Explain your point of view.

10.    How does Mother Victoria view the women?
       How does this make you feel?

11.    Is this an easy scene to watch?
       Fully explain your point of view.

12.    Mother Victoria admits to feeling as Sister Virginia does,
       as a younger woman.
       Bearing this in mind, how does her current outlook make
       you feel?

13. Does Sister Virginia show us that good people exist? Does she effectively challenge the authority of her world? Explain your view.

# Relationships

The power relationship between Sister Virginia and Mother Victoria is clear as the younger woman kneels and asks permission to dispose of a box of chocolates. Mother Victoria is the figure of authority, granting permission.

Mother Victoria asks the novice how she is getting on, interested in how she is doing. However, when Sister Virginia expresses sorrow for the women, Mother Victoria reacts negatively.

Sister Virginia bravely makes the case that the women deserve better treatment, showing that she cares about them, unlike Mother Victoria.

Mother Victoria calls the women weak, sinful, and treacherous, and warns Sister Virginia to be careful when Brigit is using bleach. She distrusts the women, despite Sister Virginia's assertion that they will not harm her.

Sister Virginia says if she were Brigit or Cathy, and had her baby taken from her, she would tear the walls down. She empathises with the women and shares their anger.

Mother Victoria is unmoved by the younger woman, citing the rule of the Church. Sister Virginia thanks her and says she will try.

This scene is marked by the power relationship between the women, and Mother Victoria's inability to really listen to what Sister Virginia has to say.

1. How does Mother Victoria treat Sister Virginia?

2. Is Mother Victoria interested in Sister Virginia's views?

3. How does Sister Virginia feel about the penitent women?

4.     How does Mother Victoria feel about the penitent women?

How does she treat them?

Include examples in your answer.

5.     What warning does Mother Victoria give Sister Virginia? What does this tell you about her relationship with the women?

6.     "They won't harm me, Mother Victoria!"

What does this line tell you about Sister Virginia's relationship with the women?

7.     How does Mother Victoria deal with Sister Virginia's outburst?

8.     Does Sister Virginia make an impact on Mother Victoria in this scene?

Explain your point of view.

9.     From what you have seen/read so far, would you describe the relationships in this play as mostly positive or mostly negative?

Use examples to support your ideas.

## Hero, Heroine, Villain

*Sister Virginia, Mother Victoria*

Sister Virginia shows bravery in this scene by challenging her superior. Mother Victoria reveals how judgemental she is, viewing the women as weak and untrustworthy.

Mother Victoria warns Sister Virginia to be careful in the laundry, saying Sister Luke has scars Brigit caused with bleach. She views Brigit as a potentially dangerous character.

1. Is Sister Virginia brave in this scene?
   Give a reason for your answer.

2. How does Mother Victoria view the penitent women?
   What does this tell you about her?

3. Why does Mother Victoria warn Sister Virginia to be careful when Brigit is using bleach?
   What is she suggesting here?

4. Does Mother Victoria strike you as a villain in this scene?
   Explain your view.

5. If you were Sister Virginia, how would you feel as this scene ends?
   Give reasons for your answer.

# Act 2, Scene 2 - Floor

The women imagine a dancefloor, before Brigit imagines purgatory, and begins to send characters there to suffer.

## Cultural Context/Social Setting

The women clean Mother Victoria's office. Mandy likens the floor to that of a dance-hall, reminding us of the social world, and men, missing from the women's lives.

Brigit transforms a dustbin into the smoke and flames of purgatory, frightening Sister Virginia. This shows the significance of religion in this world, and the emphasis on punishment and suffering this society lives by.

Brigit commits first the women and then men to purgatory. She imagines the men suffering and being punished in a way they have escaped in life. Imagining their suffering highlights its non-existence in the real world, where men are not held accountable as women are.

1. What does Cathy's cough tell you about this place?

2. "I'll speak to Mother Victoria about new equipment, Cathy!"
   Do you think new equipment is likely?
   Explain your view.

3. How does Nellie-Nora describe purgatory?
   What does this tell you about the beliefs of this world?

4. What does Brigit's imagined purgatory tell you about this world?

# Literary Genre

This scene is stylistically rich, as music, percussion, song and gesture all combine to create a dark, unsettling atmosphere, and a focus on punishment and suffering.

Cathy's attack of coughing as the scene begins reminds the audience that she is ill and makes us worry about her.

Mandy sees the floor as a dance-hall, and misses the presence of men. Her character, ever romantic, reminds the audience both of how these women have ended up here, and that they are deprived of male company, romance and love.

Through humming, drumming and a lighting change, the stage becomes the dance-hall Mandy longs for. The women's fantasies seem real, part of their lives, a momentary escape from the laundry.

Brigit throws cloths into a bin, lit up in crimson. As she throws them in, she says the bin is eating up the women. This scene is surreal and unsettling as Brigit suggests the penitents are gobbled up by purgatory.

Sister Virginia plays along, convinced by Brigit's imagined scene. Brigit asks Mandy to look in the bin to see Richard, but Mandy refuses, waltz-dancing around the stage. The women's fantasies are overlapping and confusing, disturbing the audience. Brigit tells an imaginary Mother Victoria she must go to the other place (Hell) as the music and cleaning gains momentum. Brigit speaks to John-Joe and the others in the bin, saying she has nothing to slake their thirst. This scene is both surreal and macabre, as Brigit conjures up a vivid picture of purgatory and the souls trapped within.

Note how percussion, music and movement adds to the atmosphere and energy of this scene. It is dark, disturbing and powerful.

The symbolism of purgatory and the idea of suffering before entering Heaven cannot be overlooked. Brigit imagines purgatory, while living in a state of suffering and judgement.

1. Sister Virginia does Cathy's polishing.

   What does this tell you about Sister Virginia's character?

2. "Still - nice trouble, Brigit!"

   What does Mandy's character represent to you?

   What does she add to the story for the audience?

3. How is the impression of a dance-hall conjured in this scene?

   Are these effective techniques?

   Explain your view.

4. "Bin gobbles her up!"

   Explain the symbolism here, as Brigit throws cloths into the bin.

   How has the mood changed from what it was moments before?

5. "I'm not ready for Purgatory yet, Saint Peter!"

   Does Sister Virginia sound scared?

   What is the effect of this?

6. Consider Nellie-Nora's definition of purgatory.

   What does this add to the mood of the scene?

   Could it mean anything else in the context of the story?

   Explain your view.

7. Brigit creates this vision of purgatory.

   What does this tell you about Brigit's character and how she is feeling?

8.        Is Brigit a very forceful character?

                Use examples to support your view.

9.        How does the tone change in this scene?

                What is the effect of each change?

                How does this impact on the audience?

                Is this effective storytelling?

10.       Comment on the imagery in this scene.

                How does it add to the story?

                How does it impact on the audience?

11.       How does this scene appeal to the senses?

12.       Is this scene dramatic?

                Use examples to support your view.

# General Vision and Viewpoint

Sister Virginia giving Cathy a break and polishing for her shows the kindness and goodness of people, while Cathy's illness shows the toll her suffering has taken on her.

It is difficult to escape the drudgery and menial labour of these women's lives, theirs is a life of dull, thankless, relentless work.

The women imagine a dance-hall, once again seeking to forget their lives for a moment or two.

The mood darkens as Brigit imagines the women gobbled up by the flames of purgatory, a sinister image. Sister Virginia is fearful, saying she is not ready for purgatory yet.

This is a dark turn; as Mandy waltzes in an imagined dance-hall, Brigit sends the souls of the women, nuns, and the women's former lovers to purgatory in her grisly fantasy. The combination of Mandy's romantic escapism and Brigit's imagained purgatory is jarring and disturbing.

The reference to purgatory is significant. Purgatory is intended as a temporary state, a period that will pass, a time of suffering before release into Heaven. It is the element of suffering that Brigit focuses on.

The idea of these characters consigned to purgatory, "burnin' with thirst!" is dark and unsettling. This is a troubled vision of what lies ahead for these women after a lifetime of imprisonment and drudgery. Their suffering and judgement will continue even after death, a hopeless idea.

Significantly, Brigit does not help those in her imagined purgatory, delighting in their thirst. She seems to enjoy their torment, a negative, spiteful outlook, borne out of her own suffering and frustration with life. It is only here in an imagined fantasy that Brigit can exert any power in her empty, wasted life.

1.  Why does Sister Virginia do Cathy's polishing?
    What does this demonstrate about human nature?

2.  Why is Sister Virginia not ready for purgatory yet?
    Does she sound afraid or happy?

3.  How does Nellie-Nora describe purgatory?
    What does this add to the mood of this scene?

4.  Is it funny when Brigit speaks to an imagined Mother Victoria?
    Is it grim and unsettling?
    How does this exchange impact on the general vision and viewpoint of this scene?

5.     Who does Brigit imagine in purgatory?
What does this tell you about her life?

6.     Overall, does this scene create an optimistic or pessimistic feeling?
How is this achieved?
What is the impact of this on the viewer?

7.     Is there a sense of danger or threat in this scene?
How is this feeling created?
What does it add to the general vision and viewpoint?

8.     How do you feel as the scene ends?

9.     Is this play unsettling, difficult or disturbing to watch?
Explain your point of view.

# Relationships

A positive aspect of relationships in this scene is Sister Virginia doing Cathy's polishing, trying to give her a rest. She cares about the women's health and Cathy's worsening cough.

Brigit's imagined purgatory shows how negatively she feels about some of the characters in the women's lives. Her negative relationship with Mother Victoria is clear when she suggests the senior nun is hell-bound, relishing her lack of keys, repaying some of Mother Victoria's poor treatment.

Similarly, Brigit imagines men in purgatory, and sees herself unable to help them. She imagines John-Joe, Richard, His Lordship, and even Elvis, burning with thirst. It seems Brigit feels these men should suffer too, confirming her earlier dim view of men. There is a sense that Brigit wants to lash out and hurt others as she has been hurt, a destructive comment on relationships in the text.

1.      Why does Sister Virginia do Cathy's work?

2.      What different attitudes towards men do the women express?
        What does this suggest about their relationships?

3.      What does Brigit's imagined conversation with Mother Victoria suggest about their relationship?

4.      Why doesn't Brigit help the imaginary men in purgatory, in your view?
        What does this add to the theme of relationships?

# Hero, Heroine, Villain

*Brigit*

Brigit's frustration with her life is clear, "We're the machines, Cathy!" and "Work! Work! Work! Work is God here!"

Her attitude to men is seen when she tells Mandy that no men means no trouble.

Brigit imagines not just the penitent women, but the nuns and men too, in purgatory. She would like them to suffer, and her desire to punish them shows she is angry and resentful.

Speaking to an imaginary Mother Victoria shows dark humour and spirit. Though frustrated and angry, Brigit's life has not crushed her yet. There is great resilience in the midst of her rage.

1.  How does Brigit feel about her work as the scene begins?

2.  How does Brigit view men?
    Why, do you think, is this the case?

3.  Who does Brigit imagine in the 'bin'?
    What does this tell you?

4.  How does Brigit speak to Mother Victoria in the bin?
    What does this tell you about her character?

5.  Does Brigit seem frustrated and angry in this scene?
    Explain your view.

6.  Is Brigit a funny or entertaining character?
    Fully explain your view.

7.  How would you feel about your life in the laundry, if you
    were Brigit?
    What would you do?

# Act 2, Scene 3 - Red Hearts

The women sort laundry. Nellie-Nora gets very upset and agitated when Brigit makes her wear lipstick.

Brigit attacks Sister Virginia for keeping them prisoner, saying she is like all the others. Brigit decides to escape and gets into a laundry basket. Mother Victoria arrives and sends the women back to work.

## Cultural Context/Social Setting

The women sort laundry from Galway, their task a link to the outside world. Juliet comments on it being a terrible job, it is hard work in the laundry.

Nellie-Nora smokes found cigarette butts, showing her poverty.

The women discuss men. Brigit remembers being groped as she entered the dance-hall. Nellie-Nora remembers how the men were "terrible at the back of the chapel and in the organ-gallery!" Men are described as sexual predators.

Brigit remembers her Canon standing watching at the back of the dance-hall, promising "Hell for all Eternity" on Sundays. The watchful, judgemental element of the Church in their world is clear.

Nellie-Nora warns Brigit she will be cursed for talking about the Canon like this, fully believing in the power of the Church.

Mandy and Cathy tell Juliet about dances, and the antics of men who are happy to lie to women.

Juliet says she would like to be a nun, but Brigit points out that they would not have her because of her mother, showing once more the rules and judgement of the Church.

Nellie-Nora is upset by wearing lipstick and speaks of the man who hurt her. In this world, Nellie-Nora, a victim of rape, has been imprisoned while her rapist goes free.

Brigit attacks Sister Virginia, asking her whose side she is on. She is angry about the way the nuns treat the women.

Brigit draws attention to the different ways men and women are treated and judged in this sexist world.

When Mother Victoria arrives she orders the women back to work, and sends Brigit to her office. Brigit obeys, despite her outburst. Mother Victoria's power and dominance is absolute.

1. Describe the work of the women, based on everything you have seen/read so far.

2. Nellie-Nora smokes cigarette butts she finds.
   What does this tell you about her life and this place?

3. What are men like, according to Brigit and Nellie-Nora?
   What does this tell you about the behaviour of men, and the treatment of women in this world?

4. "And they think we're the dirty ones!"
   What does Brigit's line reveal to you about this society?

5. What does Brigit say about her Canon?
   What insight does this give you into the role of the Church in this world?

6. Why does Nellie-Nora warn Brigit that she will be cursed?
   What does this reveal about Nellie-Nora's beliefs?

7. How does Brigit view her neighbours?
   What does this add to your understanding of this place?

8.    What does Mandy's second cousin, Jamsie, add to your
      understanding of how men treat women in this world?

9.    What does Cathy's "glamour-boy" story add to your
      understanding of the behaviour of men in this world?

10.   What does Johnnie in Cillnamona add to your
      understanding of the behaviour of men in this world?

11.   Why can't Juliet become a nun?
      What does this tell you about the Church?

12.   What did Mr Persse do to Nellie-Nora?
      What does this reveal about this world?

13.   How does Brigit view Sister Virginia and the Church?

14.   "Why aren't our lover-boys locked up too?"
      What point is Brigit making here?

15.   Cathy and Mandy hurry to clean the wall Brigit has
      written on.
      What makes them rush like this?
      What does this tell you about life in the laundry?

16.   When Mother Victoria sends Brigit to her office, Brigit
      obeys her.
      What does this tell you about how Mother Victoria runs
      the laundry?

17. "I always knew you were an evil woman!"
    What do Mother Victoria's words tell you about how
    society judges these women?

18. Is the laundry a violent place?
    Give reasons for your answer.

# Literary Genre

Unwashed laundry is the focus as the scene begins, it is the women's connection with the outside world, prompting them to speak of other places. For the audience, the laundry is a constant visual reminder of the women's work, and the drudgery that fills their days.

As they chat, the women's attitude to men and the Church is revealed in their conversation, adding to our understanding of these women and their backgrounds.

Brigit complains about Sister Virginia, and tells Juliet she cannot be a nun. Her negativity brings tension and conflict to the scene.

The discovery of the lipstick lightens the mood, as the women are excited to try it on. These changes in mood keep the audience engaged, and on edge, invested in the action.

Nellie-Nora's upset is dramatic and shocking. It seems that Nellie-Nora was raped before being sent to the laundry, a shocking revelation.

Sister Virginia arrives at this very tense moment and Brigit confronts her, angry about the way the nuns treat the penitent women. This moment is shocking and exciting, and highly charged with Brigit's rage. Brigit asks Sister Virginia whose side she is on, a question that may also be in the audience's mind.

Sister Virginia does not deserve to be abused like this, just as Brigit does not deserve to be locked away from the world. This is a very emotional, negatively charged moment, that adds to the themes of injustice and wrongful imprisonment.

Despite her ordeal, Sister Virginia insists that she wants to help Brigit and is on her side. The goodness of her character is clear. Brigit responds by saying she would kill her, but she is not worth it. Brigit's murderous thoughts further darken the atmosphere and increase the tension; she is reaching breaking point.

Brigit calls for her daughter as Mandy and Cathy hurry to clean the wall before they are caught. Brigit declares she is leaving, escaping in a laundry basket, an act of desperation, further ratcheting up the tension.

The last time a laundry basket was used as an escape by the women was when Brigit said they would send Mandy to Hollywood to see Elvis. This time, the basket represents danger, contrasting with the earlier innocent game.

Cathy's attempt to join in the escape adds to the tension as she and Brigit argue and scream at one another. This conflict, and their desperate escape attempt, is very dramatic. The drama is heightened by the danger they are in following Brigit's attack on Sister Virginia. They are running out of time.

Mother Victoria arrives, crushing the audience's hopes. It is very disappointing to see Brigit caught like this, her hopes of escape dashed.

The scene takes an unexpected twist and ends on a cliffhanger as Cathy takes Brigit's idea and gets into the laundry basket. The audience must wait and see if Cathy is successful.

1.      How does the unwashed laundry act as a prompt for dialogue in this scene?

2.      Is it funny when the women discuss the underpants with red hearts and throw them around?
        What does this add to the scene?

3.	Why does Nellie-Nora get upset?
	Is this a dramatic moment?
	Explain your view.

4.	The women refuse Sister Virginia's chocolates.
	What does this tell the audience?

5.	What does Brigit do to Sister Virginia?
	Is Brigit menacing here?

6.	Is this exchange between Brigit and Sister Virginia
	exciting?

7.	How do you feel, watching the exchange between Brigit
	and Sister Virginia?

8.	Brigit throws the lipstick and chocolates at Sister Virginia.
	What is being communicated through her gestures here?

9.	Cathy and Mandy scramble to clean the wall.
	What does this communicate to the audience?

10.	"I'm going out now! In the basket!"
	Is this an act of desperation?
	What is Brigit's motivation?
	Is this a tense moment?
	What makes it so?

11.	Cathy wants to escape with Brigit.
	What does this add to the scene?

12. What changes when Mother Victoria appears?
    Is this a crushing moment or did you expect it?
    Explain your view.

13. Are you surprised that Brigit goes to Mother Victoria's office?

14. Does Cathy's decision to escape surprise you?
    Comment on the imagery as Cathy is fastened in the laundry basket.
    What does this make you think of?
    Is she likely to succeed?

15. How do you feel as the scene ends?
    What, do you think, will happen next?

16. Does Sister Virginia carry herself with dignity in this scene?
    Give a reason for your answer.

17. Have your views of Brigit or Sister Virginia changed over the course of this scene?
    Give reasons for your answer.

18. What is the mood like in this scene?
    How does it change?
    What is the effect of this on the audience?

19. What themes or central ideas in the play does this scene reinforce and strengthen?

20.     Is this an easy scene to watch?
        Does it successfully involve the audience?
        Give reasons for your answer.

21.     Is this a tense and emotional moment in the play?

22.     What makes this a climactic scene?
        Use examples to support your ideas.

# General Vision and Viewpoint

The unwashed linen prompts the women to chat about the world beyond
the laundry's walls. Cathy speaks of the city she is from, a "lovely place". This
wistful moment reminds us that these women have lost their freedom.

Brigit's memory of being grabbed at the dance-hall gives the impression
that men are predatory and threatening in their treatment of women,
contributing to a negative outlook.

The women discuss men and their trickery, adding to the prevailing idea
that women are used and mistreated in this world.

Juliet says she would like to be a nun, but Brigit points out she cannot,
as her mother was a penitent. It is saddening and frustrating to see so much
denied to her because of the circumstances of her birth.

Nellie-Nora screams and becomes very agitated when Brigit puts lipstick
on her, it brings her back to when she was sexually assaulted. Nellie-Nora
was a victim of assault, and is now a prisoner in the laundry, a very troubling
fact.

Brigit brings the issue of imprisonment to the fore when Sister Virginia
arrives. She attacks Sister Virginia, venting her anger and rage against a
system that treats her so badly. Sister Virginia however, is not a bad person,
and does not deserve this treatment. This adds to the darkness and injustice

here.

Brigit berates Sister Virginia for her inaction, for not helping them when she could. Brigit insists that heaven is no good to her, she wants to live now. Her feelings of being trapped, confined and frustrated are clear.

Sister Virginia says she wants to help, but Brigit treats her with scorn, saying she would kill her, but she's not worth it. Brigit's contempt for the powers that be is clear, as is her anger and frustration. However, Brigit's anger feels vicious and cruel when it is turned on Sister Virginia. Sister Virginia does not deserve Brigit's rage, adding to the troubling outlook.

Brigit's cry for her daughter is full of grief and mourning. This is a dark, low moment for her, with everything she wants beyond her control.

Cathy and Mandy scramble to clean the wall, fearful of discovery. The authority and rules of the Church weigh heavily on them.

Brigit decides to escape in one of the laundry baskets, a spontaneous plan that shows her desperation.

Cathy wants to go too, even though the plan has not been thought through. This highlights the misery these women endure, and the risks they are willing to take for a chance at freedom.

Brigit and Cathy's arguing makes this tense moment bleaker, as each only thinks of herself.

Mother Victoria arrives, quashing any hopes of escape. She orders the women back to work, and sends Brigit to her office. Her authority is absolute and inescapable.

Once they leave, Cathy decides to go out in the laundry basket, a desperate and dangerous attempt at freedom. As the scene ends, the audience fears what will become of Cathy. It is difficult to be hopeful in such a bleak, relentlessly cruel world. Cathy however, is willing to take any risk, excited at the prospect of seeing her girls.

1.   How do you feel when Cathy speaks about her home?

2.   What was squeezing through the dance-hall door like for
     Brigit?
     What, exactly, is she describing?
     Is this disturbing?

3.   Juliet has never been to a dance.
     How does this make you feel?

4.   Based on the women's conversation, do men treat women
     well in this world?
     Is this a positive or negative comment on life and human
     nature?

5.   Why can't Juliet become a nun?
     How does this make you feel?

6.   How does Nellie-Nora react to the lipstick?
     What is going on here?
     What does this add to the general vision and viewpoint?

7.   "It's this place! This dungeon! This cage!"
     Are the women's lives hopeless?
     Explain your view.

8.   How does Brigit treat Sister Virginia?
     How does this make you feel?

9.   Does Sister Virginia deserve this treatment from Brigit?
     How does this make you feel?
     What does this suggest about life?

10.     Sister Virginia was warned about Brigit.
        Are you glad that Mother Victoria was right about her?
        What does this add to the general vision and viewpoint?

11.     "Now is what matters! We're alive now! It's no use when
        we're dead! We want to live now!"
        Explain Brigit's outlook.
        What does it say about how she feels about her life?
        How does this make you feel?

12.     "I'd kill you, but you're not worth it!"
        How is Brigit feeling?
        What makes her feel this way?
        What does Brigit's rage add to the outlook?

13.     What does Brigit's cry for Rosa tell you about how she is
        feeling?

14.     Why, do you think, does Brigit decide to escape?

15.     Cathy wants to go with Brigit.
        Does this surprise you?
        What does this tell you about the women's lives?

16.     How do you feel when Mother Victoria arrives?
        What makes you feel this way?

17.     Brigit obeys Mother Victoria and goes to her office.
        How does this make you feel?

18.     Are you hopeful about Cathy's escape attempt?

19.     Is there a certain predictability to the women's
        unhappiness?

20.     How do you expect Brigit to be treated by Mother
        Victoria?

# Relationships

The women chat together as they work, talking about men and their poor
treatment of women.

Brigit says that soon Sister Virginia will be like the other nuns, treating
the women like dirt. This suggests that Brigit's past relationships with the
nuns in the laundry have been negative.

When Juliet says she would like to be a nun, Brigit destroys the notion,
stating they wouldn't have her as her mother was a penitent woman. Brigit
takes her feelings of bitterness and resentment out on Juliet.

When the women discover lipstick they try it on, complimenting each
other. There is warmth and friendship here.

Brigit puts lipstick on Nellie-Nora, who screams and becomes very upset,
talking about being hurt by a Mr. Persse who made her wear lipstick and
perfume. Clearly, Nellie-Nora is the victim of sexual assault.

Sister Virginia offers the women chocolates. They refuse, a rejection
of her kind gesture. Brigit wants the keys, and she mocks Sister Virginia
for witholding them, for pretending to help while being like all the others.
Brigit drags off Sister Virginia's veil and throws her to the floor. Sister
Virginia is the Church in Brigit's eyes, and she takes her anger out on her.

Despite this attack, Sister Virginia says she is on Brigit's side. Her
empathy and compassion are clear as she submits to Brigit's rage, insisting
she still wants to help her.

Brigit hates the novice nun, she says she would kill her, but she is not worth it. The power dynamic of master and captive makes it impossible for Brigit to believe Sister Virginia or see her as more than a figure of authority and oppression.

Brigit calls for Rosa, her lost daughter. She is the reason Brigit longs for freedom.

Mandy and Cathy hurry to clean the wall. Although Cathy does not think Sister Virginia will tell what happened, she wants to remove the writing before they are caught.

Brigit decides to escape in a laundry basket, but refuses to take Cathy with her, despite her pleading. Their relationship unravels under stress, each is hell-bent on saving herself, on getting herself out.

Mother Victoria arrives and orders the women back to work, sending Brigit to her office. Her power and control are clear, the women immediately obey her.

Cathy decides to escape and the others help her.

This scene draws attention to how fraught the women's relationships are, and how much they want to see their children. We also see that friendship is impossible for Sister Virginia and these women, as she stands for the force that keeps them prisoner, despite her best wishes for them.

1.    Do the women get on well together?
      Explain your point of view.

2.    How do men treat women in this world?

3.    What is Brigit's attitude towards Sister Virginia?

4.    "You're gorgeous, Mandy! If only Elvis could see you now!"
      Are the women kind to one another?

Are they a cohesive group?

Use examples in your answer.

5.     How does Brigit react to upsetting Nellie-Nora?

6.     Why do the women refuse Sister Virginia's chocolates, do you think?

7.     What does Brigit do to Sister Virginia?

       What makes her treat her this way?

       Is Brigit cruel here?

8.     Why do none of the other women stop Brigit from attacking Sister Virginia?

       What, if anything, does this tell you about the women's relationships with Sister Virginia?

9.     Why doesn't Sister Virginia get angry with Brigit?

       What does this show you about their relationship?

10.    "But I want to help, Brigit! I am on your side!"

       Is Sister Virginia on Brigit's side?

       Explain your view.

11.    "I'd kill you, but you're not worth it!"

       What makes Brigit feel like this about Sister Virginia?

12.    How do Brigit and Cathy treat one another when Cathy attempts to join in Brigit's escape?

       Does this surprise you?

       What does this suggest about their friendship?

13.     What happens when Mother Victoria arrives?
What insight does this give you into her relationship with the women in her care?

14.     "I always knew you were an evil woman!"
How does Mother Victoria view the women in her care?

15.     "We'll be thinking of you, Cathy!"
What characterises the way the women treat one another? Be specific in your answer.

# Hero, Heroine, Villain

*Brigit*

Brigit laughs at the underpants with red hearts, making a joke and throwing them around.

Her comments about "fellas" shows her poor view of men, "their minds as dirty as their fingernails".

Brigit is very negative when speaking of Sister Virginia, and shuts down the idea of Juliet being a nun, reminding the group that Juliet's mother was one of them. She is brimming with resentment.

Brigit insists on applying lipstick to Nellie-Nora's lips, and Nellie-Nora gets very upset.

Brigit is forceful and mocking to Sister Virginia, refusing her chocolates and asking for the keys. Brigit pushes the nun, drags off her veil and throws her to the floor, mocking and questioning her as she does so.

Despite how Brigit treats her, Sister Virginia insists that she wants to help Brigit, something Brigit totally disregards, saying she would kill the nun, but she is not worth it. Brigit is vicious and cutting in her treatment of Sister Virginia.

Brigit calling for Rosa shows how her missing daughter is on her mind. She desperately wants to get to her, which spurs her escape attempt in a laundry basket. Her frustration is overwhelming and she argues with Cathy, wanting to go alone.

When Mother Victoria arrives and surveys the scene, she sends Brigit to her office. Despite her protests, Brigit does as she is told, and obeys her, missing her opportunity to escape.

1.	How does Brigit react to the love hearts on the underwear?
	What does this tell you about her character?

2.	What is Brigit's attitude to men?
	Include a quote in your answer.

3.	What does Brigit think of Sister Virginia?

4.	How does Brigit feel when she upsets Nellie-Nora by putting lipstick on her?

5.	How does Brigit speak to Sister Virginia in this scene?

6.	What does Brigit do to Sister Virginia?
	Why, do you think, does she behave this way?

7.	Is Brigit fair in her treatment of Sister Virginia?

8.	"But I want to help, Brigit! I am on your side!"
	Are you surprised that Sister Virginia still wants to help Brigit?
	What does this tell you about her character?

9.  "I'd kill you, but you're not worth it!"
    What strikes you about Brigit in this scene?

10. Why, do you think, does Brigit scream her daughter's
    name?

11. Why, do you think, does Brigit scream at Cathy?

12. Are you surprised that Brigit does as she is told and goes
    to Mother Victoria's office?
    Why doesn't she stand up to the nun?

13. What picture have you formed of Brigit's character by
    now?
    Give reasons for your answer.
    Is she a fun or serious character?
    Explain your point of view.

# Act 2, Scene 4 - Office 2

Mother Victoria scolds Sister Virginia for not keeping aloof from the women and gives out to her for disobedience.

## Cultural Context/Social Setting

Mother Victoria orders Sister Virginia to kneel, scolding her for not keeping aloof from the women as she was directed to. Mother Victoria's authoritative position and her attitude towards the penitents is clear.

Mother Victoria also scolds Sister Virginia for sealing a letter without permission, showing the total control Mother Victoria wields over the novice.

Mother Victoria is horrified to learn that this sealed letter invites His Lordship to the laundry. She is appalled at the idea of the Bishop talking to the "sinful women", and is even more taken aback by Sister Virginia's suggestion of writing to His Holiness.

Annoyed with the novice, Mother Victoria denies Sister Virginia permission to serve her brother's mass, or see him afterwards. As mother superior, she has the power to deny this permission.

1.   Mother Victoria orders Sister Virginia to kneel and scolds her for sealing a letter without permission.
     What insight does this give you into the rules of the Church?
     Are you surprised by these rules?

2.   Is the world of the Church a very strict place?
     Give reasons for your answer.

3.      How does Mother Victoria feel about the prospect of His Lordship visiting the laundry?
What insight does this give you into this world?

4.      Does Mother Victoria use her power justly?
What insight does this give you into the rules of the Church?

5.      Sister Virginia's brother is a priest.
What does this suggest about this world?

6.      How do you feel about "Blind Obedience"?
What insight do Mother Victoria's words here give you into this world?

7.      From what you have seen/read so far, what are your impressions of Ireland during the 1960s?

# Literary Genre

Action moves to Mother Victoria's office, forcing the audience to wait in suspense to learn more of Cathy's escape.

This is a scene of confrontation. Mother Victoria wants to speak to Sister Virginia about her disobedience. She is alarmed to discover that Sister Virginia has written to the Bishop, asking him to visit the laundry. This is a heroic attempt on Sister Virginia's part, as she tries to gain proper treatment for the women.

Sister Virginia challenging Mother Victoria and the rules of the Church, hoping to help the women, is a very positive aspect to her character.

The audience are invested in the story of these women, and are on Sister

Virginia's side, adding to the drama of the confrontation.

However, any hopes of success the audience have are dashed. Sister Virginia's challenge is ineffective, and causes Mother Victoria to block her from seeing her brother. Mother Victoria's power is overwhelming and far-reaching. Here, we see Sister Virginia denied freedom. The themes of injustice, power and imprisonment are thus to the fore in this scene.

1. Where do you see conflict in this scene?

2. Does Sister Virginia impress you in this scene?
   Use examples to support your view.

3. Where do you see Mother Victoria exerting power over Sister Virginia in this scene?
   Is this effective communication with the audience?
   Give reasons for your answer.

4. What sort of person is Mother Victoria?
   Use examples to support your assessment of her character.

5. What is the purpose of this scene?
   What does it add to the story?

# General Vision and Viewpoint

Mother Victoria exerts power over Sister Virginia, ordering her to kneel and scolding her for sealing a letter without permission. She is annoyed that Sister Virginia has written a letter to the Bishop, appalled at the idea of him speaking to the women in the laundry. Here, we see Sister Virginia's attempt to challenge the power structures in her world is easily thwarted by her superior. Sister Virginia's attempt at bettering the women's lives is completely ineffective. The futility of her attempt to do good adds to the bleak outlook dominating the play.

Mother Victoria's reaction to Sister Virginia's disobedience highlights the negative, judgemental mindset of this world, another disheartening aspect of the outlook.

Mother Victoria denies Sister Virginia permission to serve at her brother's mass or speak to him afterwards, a vindictive punishment.

The mother superior is also dismayed that Sister Virginia considered writing to His Holiness. She is shocked that a mere novice should get so above her station. This highlights Mother Victoria's dismissive attitude towards Sister Virginia, who she views as being lesser, because of her novice position.

While Sister Virginia's attempt to help the women is to be lauded as a positive gesture, her chances of success feel very remote in this place of rules and denial. There is a sense of futility to her desire to help these women in this judgemental, strict, unfeeling world.

1. "We are scarred! We, their jailors!"
   What does Sister Virginia mean here?

2. How does Mother Victoria react to the idea of the Bishop speaking to the women in the laundry?
   How does this make you feel?

3. What does Sister Virginia want for the women?
   Is this a lot to ask?

4. Why does Mother Victoria refuse Sister Virginia permission to serve her brother's mass or see him afterwards?

What does this reveal about human nature?
How does this make you feel?

5. Do you think Sister Virginia will manage to help the women?
What makes you feel this way?

6. How do you feel at the end of this scene?
Give reasons for your answer.

7. Sister Virginia challenges the world of the laundry in this scene.
What does this tell you about her character?
Is this a positive or negative aspect of her character?
How do you feel about her challenging her world like this?
Will her challenge be effective?
How does this make you feel?

# Relationships

Mother Victoria scolds and berates Sister Virginia, saying she told the novice to keep aloof from the women.

She also scolds her for sealing a letter without permission, showing the complete control Mother Victoria expects to exert. She calls Sister Virginia impudent, annoyed by her lack of obedience. Clearly their relationship is one where Sister Virginia is expected to do as she is told without question.

Mother Victoria denies Sister Virginia permission to serve her brother's mass or speak to him, despite Sister Virginia's insistence. Mother Victoria wields power over the novice, who can do nothing about it. She sends her back to the laundry, demanding blind obedience from her.

Sister Virginia's attempts to communicate with those with influence about the women have been dismissed and disregarded. Her views are not entertained at all, a negative aspect of relationships in the play.

1. How does Mother Victoria treat Sister Virginia as this scene begins?
What does this tell you about their relationship?

2. Sister Virginia says nothing about Brigit attacking her.
What stops her from telling?
What does this add to the theme of relationships.

3. "You disobeyed me again, Sister!"
What does the letter Sister Virginia has written tell you about her relationship with Mother Victoria?

4. Why does Mother Victoria deny Sister Virginia permission to see her brother?

5. Does Mother Victoria abuse her power in this scene?
Explain your point of view.

6. Mother Victoria demands "Blind Obedience" from Sister Virginia.
What does this tell you about their relationship?
What does it tell you about relationships in the laundry?
What does it tell you about relationships in the Church?

# Hero, Heroine, Villain

*Mother Victoria, Sister Virginia*

Mother Victoria scolds Sister Virginia for disobedience. She orders the younger woman to kneel, and denies her permission to serve her brother's mass. Mother Victoria knows she is the powerful, dominant one here, and she exerts her authority over Sister Virginia who has displeased her.

Sister Virginia bravely argues the women's case, wanting the Bishop to visit the laundry and speak to the women. She even suggests that she should write to the Pope himself.

Angered by her insubordination and impudence, Mother Victoria denies Sister Virginia permission to see her brother and sends her back to the laundry.

1. Is Sister Virginia brave in this scene?

2. How does Mother Victoria treat Sister Virginia in this scene?
   Is Mother Victoria a 'bad' character?
   Use examples to support your ideas.

3. "I must write to His Holiness!"
   Is Sister Virginia very naive?
   Give a reason for your answer.

4. Why does Mother Victoria block Sister Virginia from seeing her brother?
   What does this tell you about her?

5. Does Mother Victoria abuse her power?
   Use examples to support your view.

# Act 2, Scene 5 - Discovery

Sister Virginia discovers that Cathy is missing. Mother Victoria arrives and tells them to pray for Cathy, who died in the basket, trying to escape. Brigit demands the keys from Sister Virginia, who gives them to her.

## Cultural Context/Social Setting

Mandy is upset, realising her only chance of escape is to do what Cathy has done.

Mother Victoria holds complete power over the women's lives. Brigit has been threatened with "the Big House" (prison) and Juliet has been sent back to the orphanage as a result of Brigit's outburst. Mother Victoria views the women as "bad company" for Juliet, seeing them as dangerous and sinful.

Mother Victoria arrives, whispers to Sister Virginia, and instructs the women to pray for Cathy; this is how she breaks the news of her death, without concern for how the women will take it.

Sister Virginia is alarmed that Cathy suffocated, saying she needed attention for her asthma. However, Mother Victoria cuts her off, saying Cathy's death was accidental. She tells them to pray for Cathy, this is all that will be done for her in this world.

Brigit demands the keys from Sister Virginia. As she leaves she taunts the nun that, "Ye're the ones that are dead, Virginia! Dead inside yer laundry basket hearts!" Her taunts reflect the cold, unfeeling way the nuns treat the women.

The voice of Kathleen Ferrier shows the position of the penitent women in this world, "despised and rejected", locked away by society.

1.      What did Mother Victoria threaten Brigit with?

2.  How does Brigit view Mother Victoria?

    Do you agree with her?

    Give reasons for your answer.

3.  Why has Juliet been sent back to the orphanage?

    What does this tell you about how the women are viewed?

4.  How do the women learn of Cathy's death?

    Does this lack compassion, in your view?

5.  "It was an accidental death!"

    Is Mother Victoria concerned about Cathy's death?

    What does this tell you about how she views the penitents?

    Will Cathy's death be investigated?

    Why/why not?

    What does this tell you about this world?

6.  Why does Sister Virginia give Brigit the keys?

    What does this tell you about this world?

7.  Do you expect Sister Virginia to be forgiven for her actions?

    Explain your point of view.

8.  What does the song, "He was despised" remind you about this world?

9.  Is this world a very harsh, unfeeling place?

    Give reasons for your answer.

# Literary Genre

This is the final piece in the story of these women's lives before action moves to 1992.

This emotional scene follows Sister Virginia's attempt at challenging Mother Victoria.

Brigit has been threatened with prison, Juliet has been sent back to the orphanage; Mother Victoria's power is unbreakable, adding gloom to the atmosphere.

Sister Virginia arrives with broken flowers and asks Mandy to put them in water. Mandy tears the petals from them, saying the childhood "He loves me" rhyme, before tearing them all to pieces, a gesture of sadness and frustration. Her romantic hope is crushed by her restrained life.

Sister Virginia looks for Cathy, worried and agitated. This adds tension to the scene, discovery of Cathy's escape is imminent.

Mother Victoria arrives, whispers to Virginia, and instructs the women to pray for Cathy. Her whispers tell us that something has happened that the women are not privy to.

The women are shocked, asking whether Cathy got away. It is Sister Virginia who tells them that Cathy has died. The women are distressed and upset, with Brigit wishing she left herself, and Nellie-Nora not believing that Cathy has died. Their confusion and distress amplifies the sense of loss here.

Mother Victoria says the Our Father, demonstrating the constant presence of the Church in the women's lives. Her words of forgiveness and deliverance from evil ring hollow in this place of perpetual punishment.

When Mother Victoria leaves, Brigit demands the keys from Sister Virginia as the other women sob. This is a highly charged moment, with Brigit once again confronting Sister Virginia in the midst of such confusion and sorrow.

It is extremely tense as Brigit and Sister Virginia stare at one another, one desperate for escape, the other weighing up whether she can break her duty to the Church. It is a very involving moment for the audience as we hope for Brigit's escape, willing it to happen.

Sister Virginia prays as she gives Brigit the keys, hoping she is doing the right thing.

This is the moment of Brigit's escape. As she dramatically flees through the audience, she taunts Sister Virginia's prayer, "Ye're the ones that are dead, Virginia!" Her sneering tone and talk of death adds to the sense of her furious bitterness. Her escape does not feel jubilant, as the words "He was despised. Despised and rejected..." remind us.

The audience feels relief that Brigit has escaped, that she now has a chance at living her life. However, our happiness is incomplete. Her daughter visiting the laundry as the play began told us she never found her baby. Also, Brigit may be free, but the others remain. This is not a happy ending.

1. What is the mood like as the scene begins?
   Give a reason for your answer.

2. Why does Sister Virginia carry "broken" flowers?
   What does this signify?

3. How does Brigit react to the flowers?
   What does this tell you about how she is feeling?

4. What does Mandy's treatment of the flowers
   communicate to the audience?
   Is this effective storytelling?

5.  "Where's Cathy?"
    Is this a tense moment?
    Give a reason for your answer.

6.  "We must pray for Cathy!"
    Is this a crushing moment for the women?
    What is its impact on the audience?

7.  "They found her in the basket."
    Is this a gruesome or macabre death for Cathy?
    How does this impact on the audience?
    How does this make you feel?

8.  What communicates the women's distress and grief to the
    audience?
    How does this impact on the audience?

9.  "Finish the prayers, Sister Virginia!"
    What is the effect of the prayers in this scene?

10. Is it tense, when Brigit demands the keys from Sister
    Virginia?
    Give a reason for your answer.
    How is the tension created on stage?

11. Are you surprised that Sister Virginia gives Brigit the
    keys?
    Fully explain your view.

12. Is Brigit's escape the story's climax?
    Explain your point of view.

13. What does the voice of Kathleen Ferrier add to this scene?
What does it communicate to the audience?

14. What do Nellie-Nora's actions as the scene ends add to the scene?
What does this communicate to the audience?

15. How do you feel as this scene ends?
What, do you think, will happen next?

# General Vision and Viewpoint

As the women discuss the noise of the previous night, Mandy breaks down in tears. This time, talk of an Elvis photo does not soothe her, she says her only chance is to do what Cathy did. Pretence and distraction have been stripped away, Mandy's desperation and frustration remains.

The women learn of Cathy's death when they are instructed to pray for her. Hers is a poignant death, dying as she tried to escape her imprisonment. This is a sad, hopeless moment, underscoring the wretchedness, futility and waste of these women's lives.

The women are confused and upset to learn of Cathy's death. Brigit wishes she had gone herself, Nellie-Nora cannot accept that Cathy has died, saying it must be a mistake. Their distress adds to the sadness and bleakness of this scene.

In the midst of this grief, Brigit demands the keys from Sister Virginia. They face one another, staring. This is a moment of self-examination for Sister Virginia, as she must choose what is right, what reflects her integrity. Sister Virginia hands Brigit the keys, showing her strength and bravery in choosing to help Brigit rather than being an instrument of an oppressive system.

Brigit does not thank Virginia, but taunts her, "Ye're the ones that are dead, Virginia! Dead inside yer laundry basket hearts!" Brigit's grim delight dampens our feelings of success at her escape. She is free, but future happiness is not assured in this bleak world, as the words "He was despised..." remind us.

As Nellie-Nora shrouds Mandy, we are reminded that the bleak lives of the women who remain are unchanged, a gloomy, hopeless outlook.

1.  Why is Mandy upset?
    What is different this time?
    What does this add to the general vision and viewpoint?

2.  Mother Victoria has threatened to send Brigit to prison.
    How does this affect the general vision and viewpoint?

3.  "She's the one that should be in there! Power mad! Money mad!"
    Does Brigit accurately describe Mother Victoria?
    How does this make you feel?
    Is there a sense of futility to her words?
    Explain your point of view.

4.  How does Cathy's death make you feel?
    How does the manner of her death impact on the general vision and viewpoint?

5.  "Her asthma, Mother! Cathy suffocated!"
    Why does Sister Virginia challenge Mother Victoria about Cathy's death?

6. How do the penitent women respond to the news of Cathy's death?
   How does this make you feel?

7. Are you surprised that Brigit demands the keys from Sister Virginia?
   Are you surprised that Sister Virginia gives the keys to her?
   Is this a triumphant moment?
   Fully explain your point of view.

8. How does this scene end?
   What does this contribute to the general vision and viewpoint?

9. Are you hopeful for Brigit's future?
   Are you hopeful for the other women's futures?
   How does this affect the play's outlook?

10. Is escape possible for these women?
    Have they been treated fairly by life?
    What does this suggest about life?

# Relationships

Mother Victoria has threatened to send Brigit to jail and has sent Juliet back to the orphanage. Her power over the women is absolute.

Nellie-Nora says Sister Virginia did not tell on them. Sister Virginia has not gone to Mother Victoria about Brigit's mistreatment of her, showing compassion and understanding for the women. Her care and concern is genuine, and by keeping Brigit's attack a secret, she is trying to protect them.

Mother Victoria does not tell the women about Cathy's death, but whispers to Sister Virginia and instructs the women to pray for Cathy. Her approach here shows that she has no respect for the women or how this sad news will make them feel.

The women are confused, upset and distressed when they learn of Cathy's death. Nellie-Nora cannot believe that it is Cathy who has died. Her loss shows how much Cathy mattered to her, their friendships with each other are all the women have.

This time, when Brigit demands the keys from Sister Virginia, the nun gives them to her, aiding her escape. Her empathy and understanding motivates the novice to break the rules and help Brigit.

Brigit does not thank her though, taunting her instead. Brigit hates the nuns and all they stand for, even as Virginia returns her her freedom.

In this scene we see how meaningful the women's friendships are, they are bereft to have lost Cathy. Brigit's hatred of the Church that has denied her her life, is also vivid and intense in this scene.

1. Mother Victoria has threatened Brigit with prison and sent Juliet back to the orphanage.
   What does this show you about the balance of power in the laundry?

2. "The rip says we're bad company for a young girl!"
   How does Mother Victoria view the women?

3. Do the women like Sister Virginia?
   Explain your point of view.

4. How do the women respond to learning of Cathy's death?
   What does this tell you about their relationships?

5.  Why does Sister Virginia give Brigit the keys, in your
    opinion?
    What does this suggest about her relationships with the
    women?
    What does this suggest about her relationship with the
    Church?

6.  How does Brigit treat Sister Virginia when she gets the
    keys?
    Does this surprise you?
    What does this tell you about Brigit's relationship with
    Sister Virginia and the Church?

# Hero, Heroine, Villain

*Brigit, Sister Virginia*

As the scene begins, Brigit angrily rails against Mother Victoria, who has
threatened to send her to prison. Brigit's defiant spirit is admirable, but
there is a sense of futility here too. She angrily says the nuns are all the same,
showing her resentment, but she remains unable to do something to change
her situation.

Nellie-Nora says that Sister Virginia has not told on them. Despite how
Brigit treated her, the novice has not gone to Mother Victoria, showing her
integrity, strength of character and sympathy for the women.

Brigit responds to the news of Cathy's death by wishing she had gone
herself. She is hell-bent on escaping this place. She demands the keys from
Sister Virginia, who gives them to her this time.

Perhaps Sister Virginia realises that she cannot help the women in the
laundry, and so allows Brigit to escape. The novice is doing what she feels is
right, even though it is not what the Church would want. Her actions show

bravery and integrity.

Brigit does not thank Sister Virginia, but taunts her as she flees. She shows no gratitude, just hatred of the nuns who have oppressed her for so long.

1. Does Brigit sound bitter when she talks about the nuns? Would you be the same, in her position?

2. Sister Virginia has not told on the women. Does this surprise you? Explain your point of view.

3. Are you surprised that Brigit demands the keys, based on what you know of her?

4. Are you surprised that Sister Virginia gives Brigit the keys, based on what you know of her?

5. How does Brigit treat Sister Virginia here? Why does she treat her this way?

6. Are you hopeful for Brigit's future? Give a reason for your answer.

7. Does this scene change how you view Brigit? Give a reason for your answer.

8. Does this scene change how you view Sister Virginia? Give a reason for your answer.

9. Are you glad Brigit has escaped?

# Act 2, Scene 6 - Epilogue

The story returns to 1992, where Rosa speaks to Nellie-Nora.

## Cultural Context/Social Setting

Rosa was adopted when she was born and is called Caroline now. This shows the practice at the time of taking the penitents' babies and having them adopted.

Nellie-Nora tells Rosa that Brigit was sent to the laundry by her brother and that she often spoke of John-Joe from Cillnamona.

Nellie-Nora says the women never come back to visit, wanting to forget the place. In this world, the laundry is something to be forgotten, rather than confronted. Nellie-Nora is still hidden away after all these years.

Nellie-Nora tells Rosa that she does not get out much, refusing the offer of a visit to Shannon. Nellie-Nora has been damaged by this place, and cannot engage with life outside the laundry. She is a victim of this institution, and the Catholic authorities who denied her her life.

1.  "Brigit was put in here! Her brother signed her in before he got married!"
    What does this tell you about the treatment of women in this world?
    Are you surprised Brigit's brother treated her this way?

2.  Why does Rosa know so little of her origins?
    What does this tell you about this world?

3.    "I suppose they wanted to forget this place."
      Why, do you think, do the women want to forget about
      the laundry?
      What does this suggest about their society?

4.    Is Nellie-Nora a victim of her society?
      Explain your view.

5.    How does this final scene add to your understanding of
      how women are viewed and treated in this society?

# Literary Genre

"He was despised" plays, linking this scene to the previous one, but action
has moved forward to 1992, where the story began. The audience is
reminded that the fragments of the women's lives we have witnessed were
brought about by Rosa's search for her mother.

Mandy and Sister Virginia are frozen, shrouded in purple drapes. They
are a dramatic visual reminder of the women of the laundry, ever-present,
frozen and forgotten in time.

The laundry basket is a visual reminder of both the work of the laundry,
and Cathy's death. The audience is aware of the significance of the basket,
feeling involved somehow in this failed escape we have witnessed.

Rosa converses with Nellie-Nora, asking questions about Brigit,
her mother. There is sadness to this, as the audience has witnessed the
difficulties of life in the laundry for Brigit. We are aware that we know more
about Brigit than her daughter will ever know.

There is s sense of loss and sadness as Rosa searches for her mother and
Nellie-Nora cannot give her the information she needs. Her assurances that
Brigit loved Rosa are both consoling and heart-breaking, adding to the sense

of sadness as the play concludes.

It is also saddening when Rosa offers to bring Nellie-Nora out for a visit and Nellie-Nora anxiously refuses. She is testament to the effect of a lifetime in this institution. By moving forward to 1992, the playwright shows the far-reaching, lasting effects of life in the laundry.

The final image of Nellie-Nora trembling on stage is sad and moving. She is a victim of the laundry, entirely alone. Sister Virginia's voice-over tells the audience of the numbers of women who have suffered, and died, in this place. This is a dark, bleak ending, full of sadness. It highlights the injustice of this system that wronged so many women and robbed them of their lives.

1. What is the effect of "He was despised" playing as the scene begins?

2. What is the effect of the figures draped in purple?

3. What is the effect of the laundry basket on stage?
   What is the playwright trying to remind the audience of?

4. Does Rosa seem hopeful and naive to you?
   How does this impact on you?

5. "She always wanted to find you, Rosa!"
   How does this scene make you feel?

6. Why has the playwright chosen to end this story in 1992?
   What point is she making here about these women and their lives?

7. Describe Nellie-Nora as the play ends.
   What impact does she make on the audience?
   What is being communicated here?

8.       What is the effect of Sister Virginia's voice-over at the play's end?
What message is the playwright imparting?
What does she want her audience to realise?

9.       How do you feel as the play ends?
Explain what makes you feel this way.

10.      Is this a satisfactory ending?
Give reasons for your answer.

11.      Is this an effective ending?
Give reasons for your answer.

12.      Does this ending stay with you?
Give reasons for your answer.

# General Vision and Viewpoint

There is a sense of sadness and loss in this final scene. Rosa asks Nellie-Nora questions about Brigit, hoping to learn something of her mother. Her hope and naivity is poignant following our insight into the life of drudgery and imprisonment forced onto these women.

Nellie-Nora cannot give Rosa the answers she needs. There is a sense of loss and waste here over the separation of these mothers and their children, these lives torn asunder.

It is also sad that Nellie-Nora remains here. She never escaped the laundry, and remains, trapped forever.

Nellie-Nora assures Rosa that her mother wanted to find her and was heart-broken to have lost her. This is a sad, bleak reality of life, that so much was taken away, so much loss and suffering inflicted.

The audience knows that Brigit escaped, yet she never found Rosa. We have to wonder what became of Brigit in the world outside the laundry. Our questions and doubts further darken the ending, as we are left with many unanswered questions.

Nellie-Nora refuses the offer of a visit to Shannon, afraid of life outside. It is saddening that Nellie-Nora is reduced to living her days out in this institution that has taken so much from her.

Nellie-Nora, shaking and trembling, entirely alone, is the final figure onstage. Sister Virginia's voice names penitents whose remains were reburied. There is much sadness in this ending, and an overwhelming sense of loss, suffering and injustice.

1.  How does Rosa feel about learning of her mother?
    How does this make you feel?

2.  "Did Brigit talk about - going - to look for me?"
    How does Rosa feel about Brigit?
    How does this make you feel?
    Is this a positive or negative aspect of the play?
    Explain your point of view.

3.  Is Rosa hopeful about learning of her mother?
    Are you hopeful?
    Explain what makes you feel this way.

4.  "She always wanted to find you, Rosa! It broke her heart giving you up like that."
    How does loss and separation colour the general vision and viewpoint here?

5.    Why doesn't Nellie-Nora want to visit Rosa in Shannon?
      What does this tell you about her?
      How does this make you feel?

6.    Is Nellie-Nora scared of life?
      How does this impact on the outlook here?

7.    Nellie-Nora never escaped this place, nor did the women
      Sister Virginia's voice-over catalogues.
      How does this impact on the general vision and
      viewpoint?
      What is Burke Brogan suggesting about life?

8.    How have these penitent women been treated by life?

9.    How do you feel as the play ends?

# Relationships

This scene puts the separation of mother and baby at its centre, focusing on this type of distressed relationship. Rosa wants to learn something of her mother, Brigit. She asks if she is the baby in Brigit's photograph, and is disappointed to learn she is a "paper-baby", a picture Brigit adopted and pretended was hers.

Rosa has many questions for Nellie-Nora, looking for a connection with her lost mother. This shows the significance of Brigit to Rosa. Despite her absence, Rosa wants to know about her mother and hopes Brigit wanted to find her, something that Nellie-Nora assures her is the case.

Brigit is distant and longed for, just as Rosa was. Theirs is a relationship marred by loss and separation. They have been denied their bond, robbed of knowing each other and being a family.

1.       Brigit adopted a "paper-baby".
What insight does this give you into how she felt about her child?

2.       Brigit was signed into the laundry by her brother.
What does this tell you about relationships in this world?

3.       How does Rosa feel about Brigit?
What does this add to the theme of relationships?

4.       "...none of the women ever came back to visit."
Are you surprised that none of the women visit Nellie-Nora?
Is this a reflection on their friendship?

5.       "She always wanted to find you, Rosa! It broke her heart giving you up like that."
How did Brigit feel about Rosa?
How does Rosa feel about Brigit?
How does Rosa and Brigit's relationship add to the theme of relationships?

# Hero, Heroine, Villain

*Brigit*

Brigit is absent as the story ends. Rosa asks Nellie-Nora about her, hoping to learn something of her mother.

Nellie-Nora tells Rosa that Brigit always wanted to find her and that giving her up broke her heart. It is Brigit as caring mother that we are left with in this final scene.

Rosa's questions echo those of the audience. There is much about Brigit that we will never know. The final picture of her we are left with is of a mother, who escaped the laundry.

1.  What picture of Brigit does Nellie-Nora create for Rosa? Does it match the Brigit you have got to know over the course of the play?

2.  Are you disappointed not to hear what happened to Brigit after her escape?

3.  Are you surprised that Brigit never found Rosa?

# The Comparative Study

# Cultural Context/Social Setting

*Cultural Context/Social Setting refers to the world of the text.*
*Consider social norms, beliefs, values and attitudes.*

The play is set in Ireland in the 1960s. The action of the story takes place in an entirely closed environment, a convent-laundry, a place that is itself a symptom of its time and society.

Pregnant, unmarried women were signed into these homes by their families. Viewed as 'fallen women' and shunned by society, their babies were taken from them, and they were left to work in the laundry, their lives filled with drudgery.

The women are maintained in the laundry by the nuns. We see that Sister Virginia and Mother Victoria hold the keys, and thus, the women's freedom. Here, there are women in charge, and women kept prisoner. The nuns are an instrument of the male world of the Church, it is they who keep the women locked away, working in the laundry.

The Catholic Church run the laundry as a business, and performing His Holiness' laundry duties to a high standard is the mother superior's chief concern, "Work! Work! Work! Work is God here! Washing, scrubbing, washing, scrubbing, scrubbing, labouring!"

The work of the laundry is physically demanding and repetitive. The women, wash, iron, and mend. All of their work involves cleaning, preparing or repairing clothing.

This is a very judgemental world. When Cathy escapes, children mock her. Juliet, an orphan, tells the story of being attacked by the vegetable man, who saw her as fair game because she was connected to the laundry. These women are judged and looked down on because they were pregnant and unmarried, showing how intolerant their society is.

The significance of the Church in this world is very important. Sister

Virginia, training to be a nun, has a brother who is a priest - having a vocation is part of everyday life.

The Bishop is a revered figure, who is looked up to by Mother Victoria. Not only this, he enjoys a lavish lifestyle, living in luxury and jetting off to Rome. The clergy are very powerful people, due to their position in society, where so much value is placed in the Church.

The power of the Church is felt in the laundry, where the nuns are effectively prison guards, overseeing all the women do, and keeping them captive.

When Sister Virginia challenges the treatment of the women, Mother Victoria dismisses her entirely. There is no room in this world for alternative views.

This is a very sexist world. While the women are sent to the laundry for being pregnant, the men who got them pregnant suffer no ill consequence whatsoever, even when the pregnancy was a result of rape. The men walk free and continue with their lives, while the women's lives are reduced to that of inmates. They are even denied their babies, rarely getting to see their children.

Their world is a cold, cruel place, with little compassion or understanding. Sister Virginia's empathy earns disapproval from Mother Victoria, there is nothing warm or caring about this place.

Outside, people listen to Elvis songs, attend dances and watch Audrey Hepburn movies. This glamour and excitement does not exist inside the laundry's walls. The world of the women is a rigid, unfeeling one, where they are deemed evil and wicked for the sin of pregnancy.

Within the laundry's walls, the women's lives are filled with the monotony of drudgework. They are denied access to their children and are forgotten by their own families. Theirs is a world controlled by nuns, representatives of the Church, where they are chided like children and kept separate from the world.

1.  How did the women come to be in the laundry?
    Have they committed a crime?
    Who has decided their sentence?
    What does this tell you about Ireland at this time?

2.  Did these women choose to give their babies up?
    Who made this choice for them?
    What does this tell you about their world?

3.  Are the fathers of the women's babies interested in what
    becomes of the women or their children?
    Can you explain this attitude?
    What does this tell you about this world?

4.  Could the men who got these women pregnant have
    done anything to prevent the women from going to the
    laundry?
    What happened here?
    Did the women have a choice in what happened?
    What does this tell you about this world?

5.  Are the women treated as criminals?
    What does this reveal about their world?

6.  What is life like for the women in the laundry?
    Is this a boring, monotonous way to live?
    Give reasons for your answer.

7.  What is Juliet's life like?
    How does it compare to the life of a modern teenager?
    What does this tell you about this world?

8.      Why don't the parents or siblings of the penitent women help them?

What does this tell you about this world?

9.      The women often imagine they are elsewhere, doing other things.

What does this tell you about this world?

10.      Are the women treated as adults, in your view?

Give reasons for your answer.

11.      The women want to escape from the laundry.

What does this tell you about this place and their world?

12.      Have the women in the laundry been protected or mistreated by the Catholic Church?

Fully explain your point of view.

13.      Are the penitents victims of their society?

Give reasons for your answer.

14.      Are the penitent women forsaken and discarded?

What does this tell you about this world and its society?

15.      Do these women live in a fair and just world?

Give reasons for your answer.

16.      Does it seem believeable to you, that women and their babies were treated this way?

Fully explain your point of view.

What does this treatment tell you about the society of this place?

17.      Gary Culliton, writing in The Irish Times, says of the Magdalene Laundries, "thousands of Irish women were condemned to a life of servitude and confinement, with the knowledge, coercion and approval of family, Catholic church and State."
Does this statement accurately describe the world of the convent-laundry in the play?
Give reasons for your answer.

18.      If you were signed in to an institution like this convent-laundry, would you try to escape?
Give reasons for your answer.

19.      Are men punished in this world for sex before marriage?
What does this tell you about this world?

20.      Are the women happy in the laundry?
Is happiness possible for them, in this world?
What does this tell you about this place?

21.      Is this a sexist society?
Explain your point of view.

22.      Is this a controlling society?
Explain your point of view.

23.      Is this a very moral world, or simply a judgemental one?
Fully explain your point of view.

24.      How does the Church view and treat women?
Use examples to explain your point of view.

25. Briefly describe the setting of the play.
Consider when and where it is set.

26. What is the role of women in the world of the play?

27. How do men view women in this world?

28. What is the role of men in the world of the play?

29. How are children treated in the world of the play?

30. How are the women in the laundry treated in this play?
What does this reveal about the attitudes of those in authority/power?

31. Is the world of the play a difficult place for characters to negotiate?
Give reasons for your answer.

32. Is the world of the play traditional and rigid or relaxed?
Give reasons for your answer.

33. If the cultural context/social setting were different, would the penitent women's lives be better?
Use examples to support the points that you make.

34. Does the world of *Eclipsed* make it easy or difficult for characters to be happy?
Use examples to support your ideas.

35. Is marriage significant in this world?
Use examples to support your point of view.

36.      Are money, wealth, property and education important in this world?

What is valued in the world of this play?

What does this tell you about this place?

37.      What are the biggest problems facing characters in this world?

38.      What attitudes do you notice most in this society?

39.      What is considered to be unacceptable behaviour in this world?

Include examples to support your view.

Are you surprised, shocked or saddened to encounter some of the 'acceptable behaviour' in this world?

Fully explain your point of view, including examples.

40.      Is this a caring or cruel society?

Support your answer with reference to the text.

41.      Is religion important to characters in this world?

Use examples to support your point of view.

# Literary Genre

*Literary Genre refers to the way the story is told. Consider aspects of narration such as the manner and style of narration, characterisation, setting, tension, literary techniques, etc.*

## Structure

The play opens and closes with Rosa's search for information about her mother, Brigit, in 1992. The main action of the play is set back in time, in the 1960s, during Brigit's time in the convent-laundry. This action occurs as a series of glimpses into the life of Brigit and her fellow inmates during this period. These scenes show us fragments of their time in the laundry, framed on either end by Rosa's search for her mother. Due to the play's structure, the audience join Rosa in her search, beginning and ending the story with her. However, we see more of the women's lives than Rosa, who must make do with old records and Nellie-Nora's words, while we travel into a slice of their past and see these names as real people.

The play format allows the audience to appreciate each character as a living, breathing person, living the effects of society's judgements. The stagecraft makes powerful use of symbolism and imagery to have an emotional, lasting effect on the audience.

## Character

The playwright makes use of an all female cast to explore the lives of the penitent women. Five characters are inmates of the laundry, two are nuns in power. Through these characters the audience gets a sense of what life was like for these fallen women.

The inmate characters' experiences highlight the playwright's message and themes central to the story. Issues of injustice and oppression are explored through highlighting the laundry experience across a spectrum of characters, showing the ways imprisonment impacts on these women. The suffering and loss of each inmate character is clear, creating feelings of sympathy and empathy in the audience. The emotional connection the audience feels is generated by seeing the inmates live their life of suffering and drudgery.

Amongst the inmates, Brigit emerges as a defiant, heroic figure, who challenges the system that oppresses her. She is a complex character, brave and strong, but at times resentful and cutting to the other women, and Sister Virginia in particular. The many sides to her character makes her feel very real, and shows the impact on her of her imprisonment.

Sister Virginia may also be considered as a heroine, for she also challenges the laundry's authorities, and frees Brigit at the play's climax. She helps the audience to understand the women's plight, as she questions the Church's treatment of the penitents, the audience turn her questions over in their minds.

# Tension

Much of the play's tension revolves around the idea of confinement and escape, and the women's desire to be free.

The playwright effectively creates the sense of being trapped and confined, forever cut-off from life outside. She does this through conversations of lost children and life outside, the constant drudge work visible on stage, and tenuous links to the outside world - memories, letters and the dirty laundry itself. There is an oppressive atmosphere of imprisonment and confinement, heightened by talk of escape and the need to find their children. There is a sense of being contained in a place where nothing moves on or changes, relentless, limitless oppression. In this way, there is a growing tension throughout each scene, as the audience realises the extent of the women's confinement and what they have lost.

When Brigit speaks of escape and Cathy buries herself in the laundry basket, it is extremely tense, as it is when Brigit demands the keys from Sister Virginia a second time. Escape attempts are moments of high tension, as so much is at stake, and discovery could prove detrimental.

The fact that the women have been abandoned and forsaken also adds tension to the narrative. There is a sense of injustice and anger, particularly in Brigit's words of defiance and her refusal to meekly accept her life in the laundry. This sense of injustice, of society failing these women, adds to the tension seething throughout.

# Conflict

There is tension and conflict running through the play as the women are imprisoned against their will, cut off from and forsaken by the outside world.

This is seen in Brigit's anger, and her cruel words to Mandy, about how Elvis would never want her. Here Brigit is cutting and cruel to her friend, her anger bubbling over.

Later, there is conflict when Brigit attacks Sister Virginia, accusing her of being like all the others. Brigit vents her frustration at the young nun, unable and unwilling to contain herself. Thus, in the play, tension often gives way to conflict.

There is also conflict when Sister Virginia challenges Mother Victoria over the way the women are treated. The older nun is outraged and punishes Virginia for her wayward behaviour. In this way, there is conflict, not just in the laundry, but amongst its wardens too, making this a tense, exciting, conflict rich text.

# Complication

(An element that adds difficulty to the plot or conflict in a play)

A significant plot complication is when Brigit first demands the keys from Sister Virginia. The young novice denies them to her, and Brigit erupts in violent resentment. Brigit verbally attacks Sister Virginia and writes 'Scab' on the wall before throwing the nun to the ground. The other women are visibly upset as Brigit unleashes her anger. The tension builds as the audience fears discovery of Brigit's attack, and the retribution that will follow.

Tension builds as Cathy and Brigit argue over escaping in the basket, with Cathy desperate to go with her.

There is a further plot complication when Mother Victoria arrives before Brigit escapes in the basket and sends her to her office to be dealt with. In an unpredictable twist, Cathy hides herself in the laundry basket, using Brigit's idea to attempt an escape attempt.

This sequence of events, from Brigit's assault on Virginia, to Cathy's escape in the basket, is extremely fraught, with tension increasing throughout the scene due to the conflict of argument, the fear of discovery, Brigit's foiled attempt, and Cathy's unexpected escape. The pacing here works to increase the tension as events build to breaking point.

# Imagery and Symbolism

The play is rich in imagery and symbolism, from Brigit's imagined purgatory to Sister Virginia lying in the shape of the cross. The playwright's compelling use of imagery and symbolism adds depth, complexity and meaning to the narrative.

The women often engage in flights of fancy, imagining they are free, enjoying themselves elsewhere. They imagine a party in Paris for Cathy's birthday, and a trip to Hollywood where Mandy meets Elvis. These fantasies are moments of relief, but they are jarring, because they are so at odds with the women's surroundings. By imagining themselves elsewhere, they make their actual surroundings, contained and surrounded by laundry, painfully clear. The setting and props are visual reminders to the audience that no such escape or respite exists for the women. While their pretence brings moments of relief, it is only temporary, they must always return to their prison.

Cathy's cough may be considered as a physical manifestation of her situation, she is in decline because of her imprisonment, denied access to her daughters. Her illness is a visual reminder to the audience of her suffering.

The laundry basket, a symbol of the women's drudgery, is an interesting device in the play. When they imagine Mandy's flight to Hollywood, it is the laundry basket that is her means of escape. However, when Cathy dies in a basket, this idea of escape takes on a much more sinister meaning, as Cathy dies in her attempt to be free.

The basket is a symbol of the oppression that robs the women of their lives. As Brigit leaves, she tells Sister Virginia, "Ye're the ones that are dead, Virginia! Dead inside yer laundry basket hearts!" Brigit suggests that the nuns, devoid of feeling, are dead in their hearts. By referring to being dead in their laundry basket hearts, Brigit makes us think of Cathy, who died trying to escape this system, a powerful, moving image to close our glimpse of life in the laundry.

Having characters draped in cloth for the final scene is a very powerful visual effect. The women are there, but not there. They are hidden, reduced to being ghosts or shadows of themselves. Thus, the playwright suggests that they never escaped their story, forever trapped in this place from the past. This adds to the melancholic mood as the play closes, and the sense of loss and waste in these women's lives.

# Music

The playwright skilfully uses music, modern song and plain chant to create mood and add to her storytelling. Not only is the music evocative and engaging, her choice of lyrics adds to the story. For example, when the voice of Kathleen Ferrier sings, "He was despised. Despised and rejected..." it adds to the audience's sense of the loss and suffering experienced by characters.

# Resolution

Although Brigit escapes, her escape fails to feel completely satisfying. Her last words are bitter and spiteful, she does not pause to say goodbye to any of her friends. There is a lack of joy and triumph in this moment, compounded by Nellie-Nora's lack of answers in the following scene.

The audience are left with so many questions, and have borne witness to so much suffering, they are wrung out and hollow by the play's end. Viewing the play is an emotionally affecting, moving experience. The playwright wants us to appreciate what these women lost, and why. Perhaps this is why the ending cannot be happy or hopeful, considering how they have suffered.

1.      How is this story told? (Consider the play format.)
Why is the story told in this way?
What is the effect of this?

2.      How does the play's opening arouse your interest and curiosity?

3.      What are your first impressions of Brigit?
Does your view of her change as the story progresses?
Explain your point of view.

4.      Where and when does this story take place?
Be specific in your answer.

5.      The story is told as a series of fragments or glimpses, threaded together for the audience.
What is the effect of this method of storytelling?

6.      Is Cathy's cough a metaphor or symbol?
What is being communicated to the audience here?

7.      Is there a sense of being imprisoned or trapped in the play?
How does the playwright create this feeling?
How does this feeling of being trapped impact on the audience and the story?

8.      What do the women's 'flights of fancy' add to the story?
What do they communicate to the audience?
Be specific in your answer.

9. Did you expect or anticipate Cathy's death?
What does this add to the storytelling?

10. Did you expect or anticipate Brigit's escape?
What does this add to the storytelling?

11. Does Brigit's escape feel triumphant?
Explain your point of view.
What is the playwright telling us here?

12. Is this a story of relentless sorrow?
Do you feel drained as the play ends?
What is the playwright trying to show us or achieve here?
How does the playwright create this feeling of ceaseless sorrow?
Be specific in your answer.

13. What unusual features in the storytelling did you like or appreciate?
Why did you like this particular technique?
Be specific in your answer.

14. Is this play emotionally powerful?
What makes it so?
Use examples to support your point of view.

15. What is the effect of the terms 'Sister' and 'Mother' in the nuns' titles?
Does this add anything to the narrative?

16. Do you like how the play ends?
Is it a satisfactory ending?

Why has the playwright chosen to end it this way?
Be specific in your answer.

17. Is this a very serious play?
Give reasons for your answer.

18. Is Brigit a likeable character?
Explain your point of view.
Is Brigit a relatable character?
Explain your point of view.
Is she a typical heroine?
Use examples to support your ideas.

19. What obstacles is Brigit met with during the play?
How well does she deal with these difficulties?
Include examples in your answer.

20. Is Sister Virginia a likeable character?
Explain your point of view.
Is Sister Virginia a relatable character?
Explain your point of view.

21. Is Mother Victoria a likeable character?
Explain your point of view.
Is Mother Victoria a relatable character?
Explain your point of view.

22. Who is your favourite character in this play?
What makes you like/admire them?

23. Who is your least favourite character in this play?
What makes you dislike them?

24.  Which characters had the biggest impact on you?
     Explain your choices and how these characters added to
     the narrative.

25.  There are no male characters in this play.
     What is being communicated here?

26.  Is watching this play a difficult experience?
     Explain your point of view.

27.  Is the audience invested in the narrative, and moved by
     the story of these women's lives?
     Is this effective storytelling?

28.  Does the playwright have an important message?
     Give reasons for your answer.

29.  This play is based on real events.
     What does this add to the story?

30.  Is this story well-told?
     Give reasons for your answer.

31.  Does this story have a heroine?
     Explain your point of view.

32.  Does this story have a villain?
     Explain your point of view.

33.  Are props important in the storytelling in this play?
     Use examples to support the points you make.

34.     What visual techniques did you find particularly effective
        onstage?
        Use examples to support your ideas.

35.     What is the effect of music and song on the storytelling?
        Use examples to support your ideas.

36.     What were the most appealing aspects of stagecraft in this
        play?
        Use examples to support your ideas.

37.     Is the story told in a realistic or stylised manner?
        Use examples to support your ideas.

38.     Is this play conflict rich?
        How does conflict add to the story?

39.     Is this a simple or complex story?
        Explain your point of view.

40.     Who would enjoy this story?
        Who is this story intended for?
        Give reasons for your answer.

41.     Do you feel you know these characters well?
        How has the author achieved this effect?

42.     How does the author create depth and complexity in her
        characters?
        Be specific in your answer.

43.    Is there humour in this play?

How does it add to the story?

44.    Comment on the story's pacing.

Does it add to audience enjoyment, in your view?

45.    Does this play have a happy ending?

What makes it happy/unhappy?

Be specific in your answer.

Is it a satisfying ending?

Explain your point of view.

46.    Comment on the mood as the story ends.

47.    Is this a very visual text?

How does it compare with your other texts in this regard?

How does this impact on your enjoyment of the story?

48.    How does setting contribute to the story?

49.    Do you find this play to be interesting and easy to follow?

50.    What draws the audience into this story?

Highlight specific aspects of the text in your answer.

51.    Is this a realistic story?

Support your view.

52.    Is this story predictable?

53.    What themes can you identify in this story?

54.    Is this play about loss?
       Explain your view.

55.    Is *Eclipsed* an emotionally engaging text?
       Does it offer a lot of emotional depth and complexity?
       Explain your point of view.

# General Vision and Viewpoint

*General Vision and Viewpoint refers to the author's outlook or view of life and
how this viewpoint is represented in the text.*

*Eclipsed* offers an unrelentingly dark view of the world, with life full of
injustice and suffering. The women are imprisoned in a world of drudgery,
without hope of a better tomorrow.

The play creates the sense of being trapped with these women in the
laundry. Most scenes centre around laundry work, creating the impression
that there is a relentless stream of menial work that never changes. The days
run into one another, adding to this confined feeling.

Their constant talk of escape, wondering about their children and
life outside the laundry, compounds this confined, trapped feeling. The
playwright demonstrates how oppressive and constrained their lives are.
As one day blurs into the next, nothing will improve in their lives, they will
never be free. When we first meet Cathy, she has unsuccessfully tried to
get out, later, she will die attempting to escape the laundry. The women are
trapped with no say in their lives.

The women's flights of fancy also add to this sense of being trapped and
confined. When they pretend and make-believe that they are other people,
or in other places, their imprisoned reality contrasts sharply with their
imaginary escape. This sense of being trapped, unable to escape their prison,
creates a pessimistic, hopeless feeling.

Added to this bleak sense of hopelessness is the characters' unhappiness.
Characters are sad, angry and frustrated, imprisoned and forgotten, with
no future to look forward to. Brigit's rage when she attacks Sister Virginia,
and her hatred of the nuns, highlights this frustration. Brigit is seething,
bitter with resentment because of her life in the laundry. She does not even
bring herself to thank Sister Virginia when the novice gives her the keys,

but taunts her instead. Brigit's bitterness, even in escape, shows how difficult and emotionally exhausting these women's lives are.

It is sad that nobody cares what becomes of the women. Many have been signed in by their families, who are happy to consign them to the convent-laundry and deprieve them of all freedom. They have been judged and handed over into this crushing, inescapable, oppressive system. This is another unhappy aspect of the text.

The women's unhappiness is worsened by the fact that they cannot see their children. When she receives a birthday card from her twins, Cathy asks if she will ever be a mother to them, moments after attacking Sister Virginia, Brigit cries out for her daughter. This separation, and the sadness the women feel, darkens the outlook. There is a great sense of waste, loss and injustice, that these women and their children have been made to lose so much.

There is a sense that these women have been cheated by life. By becoming pregnant when unmarried, they have been cast-off by their families and society. Love counts for nothing. The men who got them pregnant have been allowed to continue with their lives, while the women live a life of drudgery and imprisonment. This feeling of unfairness adds to the dark general vision and viewpoint, where life is seen to be harsh and unfair.

A positive aspect to affect the outlook is the supportive friendships between the women. They try to look after one another. However, in moments of stress their relationships are fraught: Brigit and Mandy argue when Brigit points out that Elvis would never look at a penitent woman, Brigit and Cathy row when Cathy wants to escape with Brigit in the laundry basket. Their friendships unravel when tension mounts, as each woman fights her own corner. Also, as the play ends, Nellie-Nora is entirely alone, none of the others ever visit her. This idea of failing friendship, or friendship that cannot withstand life in the laundry, is also saddening, adding to the play's bleak outlook.

Another positive note is the resilience and strength of character the women show in enduring their lot and not giving up entirely. Cathy and Brigit in particular, are determined to escape. However, Cathy's death as she tries to escape adds darkness to the outlook.

Perhaps the most positive aspect of the play is Sister Virginia's empathy towards the women, and the way she helps Brigit escape. Sister Virginia tries to help, a glimmer of compassion in this cruel, dark place, but her efforts are thwarted by Mother Victoria.

When Brigit demands the keys from Sister Virginia, the young novice has to weigh her personal integrity against her responsibility. By choosing to help Brigit she shows inner strength, bravery and a sense of justice. Her actions here show us that good people exist, even in harsh systems, and there is always the possibility of help.

Brigit escapes, which should be a moment of triumph and joy. However, her bitter cries as she flees, and the fact that she never found Rosa, taints any happiness we may feel. She is free, but she has been robbed of her life and her baby, and we never hear of her after the laundry. Her failure to find Rosa adds to the idea that life is harsh and unfair, and that things do not turn out as we wish them to.

Overall, despite glimmers of hope, the pervading sense in the play is one of bleak hopelessness and sadness. The women are trapped forever, denied their freedom and their lives, by an oppressive system that judges them to be wicked sinners. There is a sense of waste throughout the text, their lives have been ruined, and for what? They have been left with nothing, no life, no baby, detained forever as workers for the Church. Life has been unfair to these women who lost everything. The outlook is dark and bleak, without hope or positivity. There is no escape for the penitent women. They have been wronged and discarded, forgotten about.

This sense of injustice, and of the loss these women had to bear, shut off from the rest of the world, makes this a very dark text with little hope.

1.  Is there a sense of sadness in this play?
    Use examples to support your ideas.

2.  Is life fair for characters in this play?

3.  Do you feel a sense of outrage, watching the play?
    What causes you to feel this way?

4.  Why don't the penitent women's parents free them from
    the laundry?
    What does this suggest about love and family?
    How does this make you feel?
    How does this affect the general vision and viewpoint?
    Is this a comforting or distressing message?

5.  Why are the women kept imprisoned in the laundry?
    How does this make you feel?
    What does this suggest about life?
    How does this affect the play's general vision and
    viewpoint?

6.  Do the women have any say in their lives?
    How does this make you feel?
    What does this tell you about life?

7.  Have the penitent women been let down by those who
    should love them most?
    How does this affect the general vision and viewpoint?

8.  How do the women view and treat one another?
    How do the nuns view and treat the women?
    What does this add to the general vision and viewpoint?

9.    How does the playwright challenge the morality and integrity of her audience?
      How does this affect your sense of the general vision and viewpoint?
      Fully explain your ideas.

10.   Is there a sense of being trapped in the women's lives?
      How does this affect the outlook?

11.   Is escape possible for the penitents?
      Fully explain your point of view.
      How does this impact on the general vision and viewpoint?

12.   Do the women have anything to look forward to?
      Is their hope in their lives?
      What do their futures hold?
      Is this uplifting or upsetting or depressing?

13.   Have the women been cheated out of their lives?
      Explain your view.
      How does this affect the outlook?

14.   "But I'm getting out! I'll keep trying! I'm getting out!"
      Cathy dies trying to escape.
      What does this add to the general vision and viewpoint?

15.   The women cannot pretend that Cathy has not died.
      With the end of pretence, comes the death of hope.
      Is this true for the women, do you think?

16.     How is a sense of loss and waste created by the
        playwright?
        How does this impact on the general vision and
        viewpoint?

17.     Is the sense of rage, frustration and injustice
        overwhelming as you experience the play?
        How does this make you feel about life?

18.     Is it a dark comment on the selfishness of human nature
        that these women have been forsaken like this?
        Fully explain your point of view.

19.     Is viewing the play a harrowing experience?
        Do the truths of life the play reveals disturb or upset you?
        Give reasons for your answer.

20.     Is watching *Eclipsed* an emotionally exhausting
        experience?
        Are you left feeling sad, angry, or some other emotion?
        What does this contribute to the play's outlook?

21.     Throughout the play, Cathy and Brigit never give up.
        Is the resilience of these characters a positive aspect of the
        play?
        What does their resilience suggest about their strength of
        character?
        What does this add to the general vision and viewpoint?

22.     How do characters feel about themselves and their lives?
        How does this influence the general vision and viewpoint?

23. Do characters in *Eclipsed* experience love in their lives?
    What does this suggest about life?

24. Is happiness possible for these characters?

25. Is there hope in this story?
    Will life improve for these characters?
    Why/why not?
    Explain your point of view.

26. Does Sister Virginia emerge as a kind, positive character?
    What does this suggest about life?
    Is there a positive message here?

27. How does your view of Brigit impact on the general
    vision and viewpoint?

28. Brigit never found Rosa after leaving the laundry.
    Why, do you think, is this the case?
    Did you expect a happy ending to her story?
    Give a reason for your answer.

29. As the story ends, do you feel optimistic about Nellie-
    Nora's future?
    Give a reason for your answer.

30. Are you happy with how things have turned out?

31. Do characters generally have an optimistic or pessimistic
    approach to life?
    What does this suggest about life?

32.     Is love sure to succeed in this world?
        How does this effect the outlook?


33.     What does this play suggest about human nature?
        Is this outlook positive or negative?


34.     Is life to be enjoyed or endured in the world of this text?
        Refer to the text to support your ideas.


35.     What is the message behind this play?
        What is the author, Patricia Burke Brogan, telling us
        about life in this story?
        Is this an encouraging, uplifting or depressing outlook?
        Give reasons for your answer.


36.     Do characters in the play have personal integrity?
        How does this shape your impression of the general
        vision and viewpoint of this text?


37.     How do your personal beliefs - your views and values -
        affect your sense of the general vision and viewpoint in
        the text?
        Use examples to support your ideas.

# Theme/Issue
# Relationships

*Relationships has been selected as the theme/issue to explore in this text.*

*The theme of relationships can be applied to any relationship in a text and includes love, marriage, friendship and family bonds. Consider the complexities of relationships and the impact they have on characters' lives.*

Relationships in the play are fraught and stunted, prevented from blossoming by the convent-laundry and the Church.

The women who hold the keys, hold the power, and the women in the laundry are reduced to prisoners. Mother Victoria holds absolute control over the women, she beats Cathy when she is returned after an escape attempt, and threatens to send Brigit to prison. The women are effectively prisoners, working under Mother Victoria's rule.

Sister Virginia empathises with the women and wants to help them. She even writes a letter to the Bishop, wanting him to come to the laundry, a letter which earns her scorn and disapproval from Mother Victoria, her superior.

Sister Virginia's relationship with the women is problematic due to the power dynamic of jailer and inmate. Her position as novice nun confers power on her, she is expected to run the laundry as Mother Victoria says.

This warden-prisoner relationship makes it difficult for the women to fully trust Sister Virginia, even though she makes overtures of kindness. At one point the women all refuse her offer of chocolates, she is a nun, and as such, is part of the system that keeps them locked up. This is why Brigit cannot believe that Sister Virginia wants to help her, as far as she is concerned, the nuns are all the same.

When Brigit attacks the young nun and writes 'Scab' on the wall, the women, though distressed, are all on Brigit's side. She is one of them, while Sister Virginia is not. Despite her best efforts, Sister Virginia will never be accepted by the women as she is among their oppressors, whether she likes it or not.

Brigit attacking Sister Virginia like this shows her anger and bitterness. She resents the nuns and the way they treat the women, a symptom of negative, destructive relationships.

The friendships between the women are very significant. When Brigit argues with Mandy, spoiling her illusion of being with Elvis, Cathy and Nellie-Nora prompt an apology simply by looking at Brigit and saying her name. There is a genuine closeness here, the women know one another so well that much is communicated in their looks and body language, they do not always need to speak to let each other know how they are feeling.

Also, having upset Mandy, Brigit apologises immediately. Although she upset Mandy, she tries to undo the damage straight away, with an elaborate pretence where Mandy travels to Hollywood to marry Elvis.

The women's friendships are firm, however, they are strained by the pressures of imprisonment. The tension the women feel because of their incarceration causes faults and flaws in their relationships with one another. It is impossible to always be thoughtful and kind in this environment, although many of the women, particularly Nellie-Nora and Cathy, are very warm and kind in their dealings with the others.

On a broader scale, it is important to note that the penitent women do not have meaningful relationships with their families, their children, or the men who got them pregnant. Effectively, they are cut-off from the outside world, isolated and forgotten about. They receive letters, but no visitors. Theirs is a tenuous link to life outside. They are largely forsaken by their loved ones, a very negative comment on relationships and family bonds.

1.  How have their relationships with men impacted on these
    women's lives?
    Use examples to support your ideas.

2.  How have their relationships with their families impacted
    on these women's lives?
    Use examples to support your ideas.

3.  How have their relationships with the Church impacted
    on these women's lives?
    Use examples to support your ideas.

4.  Have these women been treated well by their loved ones?
    Are they cared for and supported?
    Use examples to support your view.

5.  How do the women treat one another?
    What characterises their relationships?

6.  Do characters communicate well with one another?
    How does this affect them?

7.  Is it easy to be kind and compassionate in the laundry?
    How has this place affected the women's relationships?

8.  Who is in charge in the laundry?
    Describe the relationship between the women and the
    nuns who run the laundry.
    How do the nuns treat the women?
    How do the nuns view the women?
    How do the women view the nuns?

What positives and negatives do you see in the
relationships between the women and the nuns?

9.    Does Mother Victoria respect the women?
      Use examples to support your view.

10.   Does Mother Victoria treat the penitents with kindness?
      Include examples to support your view.

11.   What gives Mother Victoria her power?
      How does she use this power?

12.   Do Mother Victoria and Sister Virginia have a positive
      relationship?
      Is this relationship flawed in any way?
      Use examples to support your view.

13.   What strengths do you see in Sister Virginia's
      relationships with the women?

14.   What weaknesses or problems do you see in Sister
      Virginia's relationships with the women?

15.   What complicates Sister Virginia's relationships with the
      penitents?

16.   Whose side is Sister Virginia on?
      Use examples to support your view.

17.   Are these women unwanted?
      How does this impact on the theme of relationships?

18.     Brigit does not stop to say goodbye as she escapes.
Does this affect your view of her relationships with the
other women?
Give a reason for your answer.

19.     Consider Brigit's words as she escapes.
What does this add to the theme of relationships?

20.     Is there love in this story?
What prevents love from helping relationships in this
story?

21.     In this play, do characters have good relationships with
the important people in their lives?
Why is this the case?

22.     Are relationships in this text very complicated?
Explain your point of view.

23.     Overall, are relationships depicted positively or negatively
in this text?
Do relationships bring characters happiness or sorrow?
Use examples to support your point of view.

# Hero, Heroine, Villain

*'Hero, Heroine, Villain' refers to studying central characters (protagonists/antagonists).*

*Their traits, values, etc. and their ability to deal with conflict, challenges, obstacles, etc. should be considered.*

*Brigit*

Brigit is presented as a character trapped by her circumstances. She has been signed into the laundry by her brother and her baby has been taken from her. When she receives a letter, Brigit insists that she has to go and see John-Joe, her baby's father, before he marries, as he knows nothing of his daughter. She has had her life ripped from her, something that makes her angry and resentful.

Brigit is an angry, defiant, spirited character. She refuses to accept that the laundry is now her life, and is intent on regaining her freedom and finding her baby, Rosa. This is what motivates her to demand the keys from Sister Virginia, and escape out into the world.

Brigit's defiance and determination make her very likeable. As an audience, we admire Brigit's resilience, her insistence that she will get out to find her baby.

She is strong-willed and outspoken, which also shows her strength of character, "That rip Victoria! God, how I hate her!" She has suffered from her time in the laundry, but it has not broken her. She speaks against the Church and the nuns, she is not afraid to say what she really feels.

Brigit is kind to the other women, encouraging Cathy to talk about her problems, "Spit out your troubles, Cathy!" When she upsets Mandy by saying that Elvis would never look at a penitent woman, she is quick to make it up to her, inventing an imaginary trip to Hollywood for Mandy to meet Elvis. Although she can speak harshly at times, there is goodness and warmth in Brigit.

Brigit is under a lot of strain and stress, held against her will like this. We see this in the fantasy episodes, particularly when she imagines the flames of purgatory gobbling the women up, "Bin waits for your white bones, Sister Virginia!" In this scene, she delights in sending men in particular to purgatory, gleefully enjoying their thirst. This shows a desire for what she sees as justice, but also a cruel streak as she delights in their suffering, however imaginary. This is perhaps understandable though, given how she has been treated, robbed of her baby and imprisoned to work in the laundry.

Life has been cruel to Brigit. She tells Mandy, "Love is a trick!", clearly deeply affected by the way what she thought was love has led her to be in the laundry. Her circumstances have hardened Brigit, and made her bitter and cruel.

She cannot see that Sister Virginia wants to help her, and taunts the young nun, even as she is helped to freedom, "Ye're the ones that are dead, Virginia! Dead inside yer laundry basket hearts!" It is disappointing that Brigit fails to recognise the kindness and goodness in Sister Virginia, who is going against her responsibility to the Church in helping her. Blinded by her hatred of the Church, Brigit does not thank the young nun as she escapes.

Brigit's life after the laundry remains a mystery. We do not know where she went, or what became of her. All we know is that she never found her daughter.

Brigit's life is difficult, trying and sad, but she shows great determination, strength and resilience in dealing with these hardships.

1.      What are your impressions of Brigit?
Does your view of Brigit change during the story?
Give reasons for your answer.

2.    How did Brigit come to be in the laundry?
      How has this impacted on her as a person?
      Try to include a quote in your answer.

3.    What happened to Brigit's baby?
      How does she feel about this?
      What effect has this loss had on her, in your opinion?

4.    What sort of life has Brigit had?
      How has this affected her as a person?

5.    Does Brigit face many challenges and problems?
      How does she deal with these challenges and problems?
      What is your response to this?

6.    Is Brigit a strong character?
      Is this an appealing feature?
      Explain your point of view.

7.    Is Brigit an entertaining character?
      Give a reason for your answer.

8.    Is Brigit a kind character?
      Give a reason for your answer.

9.    Is Brigit a cruel character?
      Give a reason for your answer.

10.   Is Brigit a damaged character?
      Use examples to support your ideas.

11.   What three words best describe Brigit, in your view?

12.     Is Brigit the story's heroine?
        Is Brigit a typical heroine?
        Explain your point of view.

13.     Is Brigit a likeable character?
        Is Brigit a relatable character?
        Give reasons for your answer.

14.     What do you admire about Brigit?
        Give reasons for your answer.

15.     What do you dislike about Brigit?
        Give reasons for your answer.

16.     Are there things that Brigit should have done differently?
        Explain your point of view.

17.     Would you be angry like Brigit, if you lived her life?
        Give reasons for your answer.

18.     Apart from Brigit, who else could be the story's heroine?
        Explain your point of view.

19.     Is Mother Victoria the story's villain?
        Is she a typical villain in your opinion?
        What does she say and do that makes her a villain?
        Be specific in your answer.

# Selecting Key Moments

*The following is a list of key moments from the play.*
*For each moment, select which mode(s) it belongs to.*
*Write a short piece outlining what this moment tells you about this mode/adds to*
*this mode in the play.*

- The opening, where Rosa visits the laundry..

- Cathy is returned after a failed escape attempt.

- Juliet converses with Sister Virginia.

- Credo Scene where Sister Virginia struggles to pray amidst thoughts of the laundry.

- Brigit ruins Mandy's letter writing.

- The women pretend Mandy is going to Hollywood.

- Mother Victoria and Sister Virginia talk in her office.

- Brigit sends characters to purgatory.

- Brigit attacks Sister Virginia and attempts to escape.

- The women learn of Cathy's death.

- Brigit's escape.

- The ending, returning to Nellie-Nora in 1992.

# The Comparative Study: Comparing Texts

*Use the following questions to compare your texts, noting the similarities and differences between them. Include examples to support the points that you make.*

## Cultural Context/Social Setting

*Consider each of your chosen texts in your answers.*

1.  In which of the texts you have studied for the Comparative Study do characters have the most freedom and choice?
    Why is this the case?
    Justify your answer with examples from your chosen texts.

2.  In which of your texts are characters most controlled?

3.  Who holds the power in each world?
    Who is powerless?

4.  In which world is difference most accepted and respected?
    In which world is difference least accepted and respected?

5.  Which world is the least tolerant?
    Which world is the most tolerant?
    Include examples to explain your view.

6. Which world is the best to live in if you are a woman? Give reasons for your answer.

7. Which world is the best to live in if you are a man? Give reasons for your answer.

8. Which world is the best to live in if you are a child? Give reasons for your answer.

9. Which text portrays the most violent and volatile world?

10. Which of your texts portrays the safest, most secure place?

11. Which of your texts portrays the most supportive world?

12. Which of these worlds is the darkest, most fearful place?

13. Which of these worlds is the brightest, most joyful place?

14. Which of these places is the most unpredictable?

15. Which text portrays the most traditional world?

16. Which of these societies holds family in the highest esteem?

17. Which of these societies holds love in the highest esteem? Which of these societies holds love in the lowest esteem?

18. Which of these societies holds religion in the highest esteem?

Which of these societies holds religion in the lowest esteem?

19. Which of these societies holds power in the highest esteem?

20. Which of these societies holds wealth in the highest esteem?

21. Where do you see the best treatment of the vulnerable of society? Include examples to support your view.

22. Where do you see the worst treatment of the vulnerable of society? Include examples to support your view.

23. Which of the worlds you have studied is the most materialistic?
    Which of the worlds you have studied is the least materialistic?
    What makes characters have these outlooks?

24. Which of the worlds you have studied is the most secretive?
    What makes characters behave this way?

25. Which of your texts displays the greediest world?
    What makes characters have this attitude?

26. Where is love most important?
    Where is love most successful?
    Where is love least important?
    Where is love least succesful?

Compare the success of love in each of your chosen texts. What does this tell you about the worlds of these texts and characters' lives?

27. Which of these worlds appealed to you most?
Give reasons for your answer.

28. Which of these worlds appealed to you least?
Explain your point of view.

29. Which of your texts is home to the most religious or spiritual world?

30. Which of your texts showed the least religious or spiritual society?

31. How important is social class in each of your texts?

32. In which of your texts are characters most accepting of their world and society?

33. In which of your texts do characters challenge their world, society and values most?

34. In which of your texts do you see the greatest inequality?

35. In which of your texts do you see the greatest injustice?

36. Where do characters behave the best towards one another?
How does Cultural Context/Social Setting influence their behaviour?

37.     How do characters reflect the Cultural Context/Social
        Setting of their worlds?
        Explain, including examples.

38.     How does the Cultural Context/Social Setting of your
        texts lead to problems and difficulties for the
        texts' characters?
        How does it affect characters' responses to these
        difficulties?

39.     Which key moments best capture the Cultural Context/
        Social Setting of each of your texts?

40.     What similarities do you notice in the Cultural Context/
        Social Setting of this text and your other Comparative
        Study texts?

41.     What differences do you notice in the Cultural Context/
        Social Setting of this text and your other Comparative
        Study texts?

# Literary Genre

1.      Did you like the way this story was told more than your
        other Comparative Study texts?
        State what you enjoyed most (and least) about each.

2.      Is this text more exciting than your other texts?
        Consider tension, suspense, pacing, conflict and the
        author's use of the unexpected.

3.    How does the author make use of tension in each of your chosen texts?

Where is it most effective?

Where is it least effective?

Use examples to support your point of view.

4.    How does the author make use of climax in each of your chosen texts?

Where is it most effective?

Where is it least effective?

Use examples to  support your point of view.

5.    How does the author make use of resolution in each of your chosen texts?

Where is it most effective?

Where is it least effective?

Use examples to support your point of view.

6.    Are characters more engaging in this text than in your other texts?

Refer to each of your texts in your answer.

7.    How does the author create vivid, memorable characters in each of your chosen texts?

8.    In which of your texts are characters most life-like and compelling?

In which text are characters least life-like and most difficult to relate to?

Refer to each of your texts in your answer.

9.      Is the setting more effective in telling the story in this text, than in your other texts?

10.     Is this text more unpredictable than your other texts? Refer to each of your texts in your answer.

11.     Does this text have greater emotional power than your other texts?
    Was this emotional power created in a more interesting way here or in a different text?
    Refer to each of your texts in your answer.

12.     What was your favourite literary technique, used by the author of each of your texts?
    How did the use of this technique help the storytelling?

13.     To what extent are you influenced by the point of view that this story is told from?
    Are you influenced to a greater or lesser degree by the point of view utilised in your other Comparative Study texts?

14.     Which key moments best capture Literary Genre in each of your texts?

15.     What similarities do you notice in the Literary Genre of this text and your other Comparative Study texts?
    Mention specific aspects of narrative.

16.     What differences do you notice in the Literary Genre of this text and your other Comparative Study texts?
    Mention specific aspects of narrative.

# General Vision and Viewpoint

1.  Is life happier and fuller for characters in this text than in your other Comparative Study texts?
    Explain your point of view fully.

2.  Do characters in this text face more obstacles and difficulties than in your other texts?
    Who struggles most?

3.  Are characters in this text rewarded more for their struggles than in your other texts?
    Do they overcome adversity and achieve true happiness and contentment in a way that is not realised in your other texts?

4.  How do events in these texts, and your personal response to these events, help your understanding of the General Vision and Viewpoint of these texts?
    Include specific examples in your answer.

5.  How does your attitude to central characters help shape your understanding of the General Vision and Viewpoint of your chosen texts?
    Include specific reference to your chosen characters in your answer.

6.  What aspects of this text did you respond to emotionally?
    How does this help your understanding of the General

Vision and Viewpoint of the text?

How does this compare to your other texts?

7.      Is this the brightest, most hopeful and triumphant text you have studied?

Explain why its message is more or less positive than in your other texts.

8.      Which of your chosen texts was the bleakest and most upsetting or depressing?

Explain what made it more negative than your other texts. What made them more positive?

9.      Plot your three texts on a scale of one to ten from darkest (most pessimistic) to brightest (most optimistic). Add a note to explain their positions.

10.     Which key moments best capture the General Vision and Viewpoint of each of your texts?

11.     What similarities do you notice in the General Vision and Viewpoint of this text and your other Comparative Study texts?

12.     What differences do you notice in the General Vision and Viewpoint of this text and your other Comparative Study texts?

13.     Can you relate any aspect of this text to your own life experience?

If so, how does this help to shape your understanding of the General Vision and Viewpoint of this text?

# Theme/Issue - Relationships

1.   Are relationships in this text more positive and
     supportive than the relationships in your other
     chosen texts?
     Include specific examples in your answer.

2.   Rank the relationships you have studied in your various
     texts from most positive (score of 10) to most negative
     (score of 1).
     Add a note explaining your choices.

3.   Are relationships in this text the most engaging and
     interesting that you have studied?
     Explain your choice.

4.   Rank the relationships you have studied in your various
     texts from the most interesting (score of 10) to the least
     interesting (score of 1).
     Add a note explaining your choices.

5.   How do the events of the text impact on the characters'
     relationships with one another in this text and your other
     chosen texts?
     Who is most affected?
     Who is least affected?

6.   How does conflict impact on the relationships of
     characters in this text and your other chosen texts?
     Who is most affected?
     Who is least affected?

7.  How does social class impact on the relationships of characters in this text and your other chosen texts?
    Who is most affected?
    Who is least affected?

8.  Is the theme of relationships portrayed in an idealistic or realistic way in each of your chosen texts?

9.  Did any aspect of the theme of relationships shock or surprise you in your three chosen texts?
    Use examples from your texts to support the points that you make.

10. What are the most interesting aspects of the theme of relationships in each of your chosen texts?

11. Which text taught you most about relationships?
    Refer to each text in your answer.

12. Which key moments best capture the theme of relationships in each of your texts?

13. What similarities do you notice in the theme of relationships in this text and your other Comparative Study texts?

14. What differences do you notice in the theme of relationships in this text and your other Comparative Study texts?

# Hero/Heroine/Villain

*Consider the following list of questions for a central character in each of your chosen texts.*

1. Who is the most interesting character in the text?
   What makes them interesting?
   What do you like about them?
   What do you dislike about them?
   What are this character's strengths?
   What are this character's weaknesses?

2. How does this character cope with conflict?

3. How does this character cope with the unexpected?

4. Are they a resourceful character?

5. Are they an emotional character?
   Use examples to support your view.

6. Do you empathise with this character? Why/why not?

7. What do you admire about this character?

8. How well does this character relate to and interact with other characters?
   Include examples to support your points.

9. Is this character happy or sad?

10. Are they an active or passive character?
    How do they contribute to the action and storyline of the text?
    Are they important to the story's plot and development?

11. Is this character a good (successful and interesting) main character?

12. Would you like to meet this character?
    If you met them, what would you talk about?

13. If you had any advice for this character, what would it be?

14. Does this character make the story more exciting?
    In what way do they do this?

15. Is this character a hero/heroine or a villain?
    Explain your choice.

16. Identify the key moments in the text that illustrate your chosen character's personality traits/character.

17. On a scale of one to ten (with one being extremely heroic and ten being an evil villain), where would you place your chosen character?
    Give reasons for your choice.
    Where would you place the main characters from your other texts?
    Why would you place them here?

18. Which of your chosen characters do you like and admire most?

What makes them your favourite character?
Give reasons for your answer.

19. Which of your chosen characters do you dislike most?
Explain why you like some more than others.

20. Which of your chosen characters shocked you most?
Give reasons for your answer.

21. Which of your chosen characters impressed you most?
Give reasons for your answer.

22. Which of your chosen characters did you feel most sorry for?
Give reasons for your answer.

23. Who is the most resourceful character you have come across?
Give reasons for your answer.

24. Which of your chosen characters faced the most problems and difficulties?
Did they cope well with these problems?

25. How is your favourite character similar to the characters in your other texts?

26. How is your favourite character different to the characters in your other texts?

27. Choose key moments from each of your texts to highlight your characters' strengths and weaknesses.

Lightning Source UK Ltd.
Milton Keynes UK
UKHW021522011021
391503UK00007B/183